Portraits From Life

A Poet's Mentors

George Franklin

Portraits From Life
George Franklin

Published by: Nicasio Press,
            Sebastopol, California
            www.nicasiopress.com
Cover Design: Constance King Design

ISBN: 978-1-7375814-5-1

In Memory of Robert Fitzgerald

Table of Contents

PREFACE

1.

This book is in part a species, or subspecies, of the genus memoir. It involves aspects of the autobiography of an unknown, or little known, poet. Its first section, "Same Heartedness: Portraits From Life," proceeds, at first mostly by indirection, dwelling not on myself, its author, who can lay no particular claim on your attention, but on my experience of others, and on my experience as a poet and as a reader of poetry.

It pays tribute to an extraordinary series of exemplary artists whom I have been privileged to know. Two of these figures, the poet Marie Ponsot and the poet and translator Robert Fitzgerald, I encountered in classroom settings, though in the case of Fitzgerald, our bond was deepened by regular visits during office hours that he generously encouraged me to attend.

Several others—the novelist William Maxwell, the dancer Erick Hawkins, and the avant-garde composer Lucia Dlugoszewski—were friends of my parents. I encountered them as a child and grew to know them more closely in later years.

From all of these figures, I came to absorb some sense of what the vocation of an artist, when honorably pursued, entails. From the writers among them, I learned that closely attending to and listening to works of literary art, whether as a writer or reader, can, through a refining of the sympathetic imagination, which I call *felt intuition,* lead to a closer alignment with oneself, with others, and with the world that we share. Felt intuition, too, can help open up imaginative vistas, disclose spaces of enhanced possibility, of unencumbered freedom, that then, as though inevitably, transform our comportment toward our quotidian lives and to the challenges with which they confront us.

From all of these artists, I have learned of the importance of attending to that which even the most well-chosen, resonant words, the most expressive, exorbitant, and skillfully executed physical gestures, the most beguiling, enthralling, or overwhelming arrangements of notes, can never quite express, but which it is the burden and joy of the artist, nevertheless, to *try* to express.

From all I have learned the importance of cultivating an awareness of the silence and of the clear, open space that is the background against which words, gestures, and notes can alone become articulate, a background from which they arise and into which they subside.

Each of the artists to whom I have attempted to pay homage possessed, of course, unique and characteristic gifts, and developed unique and characteristic ways of expressing them. In what follows I have attempted to do justice to this particularity.

Each of my exemplary figures, of course, had different backgrounds, drew upon different streams of experience, had different temperaments, different ways of being in the world, different flaws. None were saints. And my portraits of them are not hagiographies. I do not shy away from writing about what I perceive to be some of their limitations. Nevertheless, each is a figure whom I came to revere—an attitude that is perhaps too little expressed in our culture.

2.

The second section of this book deals with my changing attitude over time to Robert Lowell, who taught at Harvard while I was an undergraduate there. It is in its own way as personal as the essays that precede it.

As an artist, one learns not only from artists for whom one has an affinity but also from those for whom one feels a strong antipathy. My initial attitude toward Lowell's work was one of something close to revulsion. He came from a social milieu, or more simply from a class, which was quite uncomfortably similar to that of my parents. My own instinct was to conceal my privileged background, a background that had granted access to several of the exemplary figures discussed in this book, but toward which I felt considerable ambivalence—an ambivalence which Lowell, to some degree, shared. On the one hand, he traded on his name. On the other, his poems about his parents, particularly about his father, had a kind of reptilian cruelty that I found unforgivable.

By the time I was an undergraduate, the WASP hegemony was just beginning to be on the wane. As a gay man, I felt like an outsider and had no wish to be burdened by an additional stereotype—one which, moreover, I felt, perhaps naively, did not fit me. I had loathed the pinched, parochial ethos of the boarding schools, breeding grounds for the WASP elite, to which I had been packed off, initially at the age of twelve, for traditional and sometimes brutal rites of passage.

Over time, however, I came, at first grudgingly, to appreciate Lowell's work and the considerable courage, in the face of mental illness, that it took to produce it. My coming of age as a poet coincided with the heyday of the confessional school of poets, of which Lowell was a leading light. Again, my own initial and continued impulse as a poet was *not* to mine the details of my life; my affinities as a poet lay with the more reticent Elizabeth Bishop and with Wallace Stevens. The essay "Coming to Terms With Robert Lowell" attempts, nevertheless, something like an informal critical reappraisal of Lowell's work. Though I still regard Bishop as the greater poet, I now regard Lowell's work as being perhaps too much in eclipse.

The first of the three related essays in this section, "Disowning Lowell," deals with my initial antipathy to him and his work. The second, "Interlude: Hearing

Confession," addresses tangentially a number of poets associated with the confessional school. In the mid-seventies of the last century, Cambridge and Boston were among the epicenters of American poetry. I hope, in this brief essay, to have captured something of the vitality of that milieu. The third and final essay, "Coming to Terms with Lowell," is written from the vantage point of my later, more mature assessment of Lowell.

In part, my growing appreciation of Lowell over the years has been due to the fact that I, like he, and like my father and grandfather, have suffered from recurrent bouts of depression and have direct experience of the ravages that such an affliction can entail.

3.

All of our lives are woven of different threads, some lighter, some darker, some more prominent, some less so, and new threads, of course, keep being introduced into the fabric. We hope that the tapestry we are creating is in some way meaningful, and that it will perhaps be even more meaningful when we are finally finished with it. But the possible experience of meaninglessness, and of what it, too, might have to teach us, must also be entertained.

Our lives, like poems, or portions of them, are, in the words of the poet John Ashbery, like "diagrams sketched on the wind." What I offer here are several such diagrams. I have attempted to faithfully execute them. They are now definitively out of my hands.

If I have one wish, it is that none of the exemplary figures—including Lowell— whom I have discussed in this text, though I have written neither panegyrics nor hagiographies, would find fault with it.

If I were to have another, it would be that this text might provide one small thread that can be constructively and productively introduced into the fabric of the lives of whoever might encounter it and might wish to read it.

1. SAME-HEARTEDNESS: PORTRAITS FROM LIFE

~ Chapter One ~

Portraits from Life

1. Marie Ponsot

1.

A number of years ago, when I was in my early fifties, I decided to take a poetry-writing workshop. I made this decision with little hope of feeling truly inspired by such a course. But writing is a lonely process, and I felt that participating in one last workshop might at least serve as some kind of antidote to that loneliness. I had taken many such courses before, both in the early- to mid-seventies at Harvard and, after a gap of several years, at Brown, where I received an MFA, and finally, after a gap of many more years, at Columbia, where I spent two years pursuing an MA in English Literature. I had come, over the years, after a promising start as an undergraduate, to find these workshops less and less useful.

Hence my low expectations when I enrolled in a class that turned out to be an exhilarating and revelatory experience. I will, of course, return to that experience but will first briefly limn my prior history with poetry workshops, in the hope that the contrasts between them and the class into which I stumbled many years later will prove instructive.

When I was an undergraduate and a fledgling poet, the students in any given poetry workshop I joined largely overlapped with those in previous workshops, forming a loose cadre, a kind of peer group, a small, eccentric society or cenacle, of which I was happily a member. Identifying with such a group served as a vital antidote to the impersonal entity called Harvard, of which I was nominally, statistically, a member, an entity which displayed little interest in the intellectual or psychic well-being of its undergraduates, who were left to their own sometimes makeshift and inadequate devices. Many, suffering the trauma of no longer being seen as exceptional, engaged (unlike those who refused to be engaged at all) in a ruthlessly competitive Darwinian struggle not merely to survive, which was easy enough, but to continue to be recognized by others and to see themselves as in some way exceptional. As I had rarely, or seldom, been seen as particularly exceptional, and as I was what is now termed a "legacy" admission to Harvard (a legacy that I took great pains to hide), I had, until I discovered a gift for poetry, inevitable insecurities about my institutional legitimacy. I was fortunate that since the members of poetry workshops tended to be friends, or at least potentially acquaintances, the atmosphere of these classes was unusually, and happily, collegial and congenial.

...And yes, I studied with Elizabeth Bishop. A small cottage industry of essays by her former students has cropped up over the years since her death. Recently, a full-length book by one of these students appeared. As it was given to me as a present, I felt obliged to skim through it. The author annoyingly refers to Miss Bishop as *Elizabeth*, something none of us, back in the day, would have been caught dead doing.

To give some sense of how zealously Miss Bishop guarded her privacy, I can report on a rather intense exchange, or rather a monologue, at the receiving end of which was a young poet friend of mine. Apparently, he had been given Miss Bishop's home phone number by William Alfred, the longtime playwright in residence at Harvard who had produced one slightly notable play, "Hogan's Goat," many years before I had even less notably materialized on campus. My friend had wanted to get some clarification about a paper that had been assigned by Miss Bishop, whose office hours were few and far between. In what was for him an uncharacteristic act of indiscretion, he availed himself of the opportunity to call Miss Bishop at home. When she realized she was speaking with a student, an intense, intemperate screed ensued:

> HOW did you get my private number! You are NEVER to use this number again! NEVER give this number to anyone else. If you have any questions for me, PLEASE bring them up them in class!

And so on. To be fair, Miss Bishop later apologized to my friend—who fortunately had a robust sense of his own worth— while still making it clear that her private phone number was off limits.

In general, Miss Bishop was baffled and put off by the long-haired, apparently unwashed hordes who constituted my generation. During the year I took her class, I had allowed my hair, which turned out to be surprisingly curly and riotously unruly, to grow out. For a few years in the early seventies, it was fashionable for white students of a certain ilk to wear—in what would now be considered on some college campuses at best as a case of cultural misappropriation, at worst an instance of micro-aggression—cheap knockoffs of *dashikis*, brightly colored and patterned shirts of West African provenance. The one that I occasionally sported had a vastly oversized, strikingly crimson (though not exactly Harvard crimson) heart emblazoned at its center. I was wearing my heart, as it were, not on my sleeve, but somewhat redundantly on my chest. My long hair and sartorial choices would not have endeared me to Miss Bishop. The few students with whom she did develop minimal relationships were mostly well-scrubbed, relatively conservative types.

It is somewhat surprising, then, that Miss Bishop, whose poems were anything but confessional, was an occasional drinking buddy of the charismatic and at times luridly confessional poet Anne Sexton, who felt a particular affinity for my long-haired peers, and who had even formed with several of them a rock band called "Her Kind," of which she was the lead singer. Almost as surprisingly, it has since become known, in what is apparently not merely an urban legend, that on several occasions Miss Bishop shared joints with John Ashbery, who was a great admirer of her work, and who was influenced by it in ways that are too-little recognized. A touching reticence, anything but confessional, is characteristic of the writing of both.

It was clear to all of her students that teaching was not simply an indifferent but a genuinely painful experience for Miss Bishop. I have no wish to give an account of her pedagogy here. At the time I considered her, presciently, taking what was then a minority position, the greatest living American poet. It did not matter that she displayed, with few exceptions, little or no interest in her students. Why should she have? Most of us need to find some way of making a living, and we are not obligated to enjoy it. I simply felt honored to be in Miss Bishop's company. I *still* feel honored to have been in her company.

It occurs to me that there is one rather charming anecdote regarding Bishop that I can report without suggesting that I knew her better than I did. The first time I saw her, she entered the unprepossessing basement classroom we would share, with one arm supported by a bulky and uncomfortable-looking sling. A small and physically fragile woman, she looked somewhat like an injured bird who had fallen out of a nest. She told us matter-of-factly that the day before she had strained a ligament in her shoulder, and that as a result she was on a brief regimen of painkillers that had left her more than a little woozy—so woozy, she said, that on the morning of the class, attempting to send a letter, she had affixed a stamp to the center of an envelope and written the address of its would-be recipient in the upper right hand corner. If she were to wax incoherent, she let it be known, the drugs, not she, would be to blame.

There is something in the quirkiness, the dry humor, and the slightly surreal quality of this anecdote that reminds me of two of the many kinds of poems Bishop wrote. A strain of bemused, observant humor is evinced, for example, in her poem from *Questions of Travel* on a valiantly derelict, obviously family-owned Brazilian gas station, "The Filling Station," which concludes:

> Somebody embroidered the doily.
> Somebody waters the plant,
> or oils it, maybe. Somebody
> arranges the rows of cans

so that they softly say:
ESSO—SO—SO—SO
to high-strung automobiles.
Somebody loves us all.

The slightly surreal quality mentioned above had surfaced in earlier poems such as "The Weed" or "The Man-Moth," never to entirely disappear from her work. "The Man-Moth," a poem that was suggested to Bishop by a newspaper misprint for the word *mammoth*, is an ineffably, almost unbearably, sad poem, imagining the haunts of a fragile, hybrid creature who keeps mostly out of sight, who rides all night, facing backward, in the vast underground netherworld of the New York City subway system, but who makes occasional, rare, clandestine, nocturnal visits, as though coming up for air, to the surface of the world in which we habitually move. The poem concludes with a stanza that imagines the hypothetical capture of this creature:

If you catch him,
hold up a flashlight to his eye. It's all dark pupil,
an entire night itself, whose haired horizon tightens
as he stares back, and closes up the eye. Then from the lids
one tear, his only possession, like the bee's sting, slips.
Slyly he palms it, and if you're not paying attention
he'll swallow it. However, if you watch, he'll hand it over,
cool as from underground springs and pure enough to drink.

The man-moth seems somehow a figure for the poet, and his or her gift, bestowed only on the patiently attentive, seems a distillate of poetry itself, one which both nourishes and homeopathically stings.

Again, it was an honor, a sufficient gift, simply to have been in the company of such a poet.

2.

The poetry workshops I took while a graduate student have all been unfairly melded into one in my memory. They followed a more or less uniform format. Copies of recent samples of each student's work were handed out. As many poems as possible were discussed in the usual hour and a half allotted to such classes. When the time came to give feedback on one of these poems, the procedure, likewise, was dishearteningly uniform. Particular local images or lines in a poem were peremptorily judged either weak or strong, with scant reference to the poem as whole. Some attention was also paid to enjambment. Thus: "this image is weak, that image is strong; this line is weak, that line is strong; this line break is clever, that line break feels forced." The ubiquitous word *image*, as applied to poems, despite Robert Bly's popularization of what he calls the "deep image," seems to me to be a kind of place-filler that means, unlike long-recognized rhetorical tropes such as metaphor and metonymy, next to nothing. Lines of poems also mean next to nothing when considered apart from the larger syntactical structures of which they are a part, which, in turn, mean little when not considered in relation to other such structures in the poem and to the poem as a whole.

But I am being needlessly technical and pedantic. What I am trying to convey is that when poems are read or listened to—or are in fact *not* really read or listened to —with a mindset requiring a rush to judgement about particular lines or images, the result often seems pointless. Imagine saying *of* and *to* a person—"Your right arm is a little long, but your left seems just right. I like your feet, but I find your hands regrettable. Your voice is annoyingly high-pitched, but your vocabulary is impressive," etc., etc. And imagine being expected to find such observations useful or helpful, when one's natural response, of course, is simply to find them hurtful.

The poet, so considered, is unlikely to feel genuinely acknowledged, but rather politely dismembered and dismissed. And yet all involved in this process genuinely intend to be helpful, and imagine that they *are* being helpful. Meanwhile, the air in the room in which such exercises are conducted comes to feel deadened and stifling. When a particular session is over, one feels little interest in returning to the theater of such operations, just as one feels little interest in returning to a particularly dull exhibition in a poorly ventilated museum.

We seldom, it seems to me, particularly in the epoch of tech, take the time to truly *listen* either to each other or to the past. Even in places or situations where one might have imagined that listening is encouraged, it is too often, if inadvertently or unconsciously, circumvented.

After this somewhat circuitous preamble, it is time to return to my seemingly quixotic decision to enroll in one last poetry workshop. Billed as "advanced," it was to be held at the New School in New York. I submitted several poems and made the cut. The teacher was to be the poet Marie Ponsot, whose name I had heard. I even recalled having read and enjoyed several of her poems. Looking her up on Wikipedia, I did the math and realized that she was eighty-eight years old. I am ashamed to say that I felt somewhat disheartened by this fact. I wondered how much energy and mental sharpness she would be able to bring to the enterprise at hand.

Further research uncovered the fact that there was a twenty-five-year gap between the publication of her first book of poetry and that of her second. In the interim, she had become the mother of seven children, one girl followed by a convoy of six boys. At some point, while her children were still young, she was divorced from her husband, a French painter who was able to offer precious little in the way of financial assistance. Marie (and yes, she encouraged us to call her *Marie*) supported herself and her children by translating numerous books, including the fables of La Fontaine, from the French, and by becoming a teacher. Finally, after her children had grown and she was freed of the day-to-day exigencies of being a single parent, she returned to writing poetry. (In fact, she had never really stopped, but she was now able to give writing more ample attention.) As a result, the second of what turned out to be a number of books of poems was published when she was almost sixty.

I found all of this quite remarkable. I purchased her book *Springing*, which includes both selected and new poems, and read it with great interest. It was soon apparent to me that Marie was among the few living American poets who had produced a first-rate and original body of work. Why had I not heard of her, or heard of her more often?

The nine of us who were enrolled in Marie's class arrived early in the seminar room in which it was to be conducted. Marie appeared exactly on time. I first noted that she was only a little over five feet tall. A large yellow button like a sunflower with the message STILL AGAINST WAR in bold black lettering was pinned to her shirt. As she sat down, I noticed her strikingly blue eyes as they took us all in. They were not just blue, but piercingly, intelligently blue.

Birds make not-infrequent appearances in Marie's poems, and there was something quick, alert, avian, yet still down-to-earth about her presence. I have forgotten what she first said, but I remember it was said with her slightly clipped but uncannily clear and precise diction. Each word seemed to be scrupulously, carefully chosen. It struck me that it was going to be an aesthetic pleasure to have an opportunity to listen to this elegant, concise, and distinctive voice at greater length.

A forcefield of energy surrounded Marie, as is the case with any charismatic person. Her presence exuded, or commanded, authority. A gentle authority, as it turned out. Within no more than thirty seconds after her entrance, all of my foolish worries about her age had vanished.

At some point, probably toward the beginning of the first class, Marie said that she could think of no more pleasurable way of spending two hours than listening to a batch of freshly-minted poems, and that she felt privileged to have the opportunity to do so. She said it, and she meant it. She clearly had a real vocation for teaching, similar in kind if not in importance to her vocation as a poet.

She then previewed what was to be the three-part structure of each of our six two-hour classes. For the first section of the class, each of us would bring a copy of a newly written poem. Each of us would read his or her poem aloud and would be asked to comment briefly on the poems of our peers. Only *after* all the poems were read aloud were copies of them to be passed out to fellow students and to Marie.

Thus, our first exposure to these poems occurred through an act of attentive listening, not of cursory reading, which is to say it happened by way of the receptive ear, not by way of the usually domineering eye/I. Before the next class, we were to write additional observations on each of the eight copies of poems that had been handed out to us subsequent to their having been read aloud. At the beginning of the next class, we were to return these observations on individual poems to their authors, who thus received nine pages of written comments, including a similar annotated page from Marie.

At the outset of the second portion of the class, Marie would hand out to us a poem or group of poems that she would briefly comment upon, after which she would invite all of us to join in the discussion. Among the poems and poets Marie selected, some were relatively familiar, including Donne's "A Valediction Forbidding Mourning" and Blake's "Proverbs of Hell" from *The Marriage of Heaven and Hell,* while others, such as a section or two from one of H. D. 's little-read and underrated longer poems, were less familiar. Still others, like a batch of Djuna Barnes' poems, were entirely unfamiliar, at least to me. I knew Barnes as the author of the extraordinary novel *Nightwood,* set in the demimonde of Paris before the outbreak of the Second World War. I had no idea that she wrote poetry.

In the final section, for the remaining hour or so of the class, we would focus on listening more concentratedly and at greater length to poems of only two students. Observations of these poems were furiously, extemporaneously, and in real time, scribbled down and then delivered orally, at some length, to each of the two poets in question. Once again, only after the poems had been thus discussed were hard copies handed out to Marie and to the other members of the class. In this portion of the class, the stakes involved in listening were raised even higher. One did not wish to deliver fatuous or threadbare observations about the poems in question and as a result, one listened to them especially hard.

Finally, Marie let us know her one ground rule for the class, to which as much as possible we were to adhere: *Our responses to poems should consist only of simple, direct observations, and should never contain value judgements.* This ground rule might at first seem to enshrine a kind of post-New Age excessive solicitude with respect to the tender feelings of others. In fact, I would find out, it did nothing of the kind. The impact it had on the class was to be extraordinary.

As should be self-evident from the above, Marie's class—I am convinced deliberately, though she never discussed with us her pedagogy—encouraged the art, or the act, of listening, a reorientation that resulted from her one stringent guideline for the course. Just observations. No value judgements. No more "this image works, that image doesn't work; this line break works, that line break doesn't." As we were not responding to poems intent as predatory animals to pounce upon them, thereby providing dubious insights—or rather value judgements, not insights—as to the high and low points of the works in question, we were instead *listening* to each poem generously, as a whole, attempting to take in, and then to set down, in the form of simple observations, as much as we could about it.

When it became time in the last portion of the class both to deliver one's own oral reports and to listen to those of others, the result, as I have suggested, was remarkable. The ad hoc observations of my fellow classmates to poems that they had just heard were not only surprisingly detailed but also, almost without exception, exceptionally perceptive and insightful. Something in our responses themselves that had never before been given the opportunity of manifesting itself had suddenly been liberated. After eight such responses had been delivered, layer after layer of the poem in question had been excavated and revealed.

When it came time to read a poem of my own, listening to my classmates' observations about it was likewise a revelatory and liberating experience. Not only was the essence of what I had hoped to convey in the poem confirmed by these responses, but I was made aware that things were incontestably there in the poem that I had never realized were present, that I had never, as it were, consciously put there, which confirmed for me that when writing poems, one is sometimes tapping into a dimension that far exceeds whatever intent—or attempt to avoid an intent— one imagines is guiding one.

Most importantly, I felt as though for the first time something that I had written had been truly heard. At the same time, more globally, I felt as though *I* had been heard, an experience that was both unexpected and moving.

The atmosphere of the class as a whole, in which all involved were both truly listening and truly being heard, was extraordinary. It was almost like being in a temple. This atmosphere was reverent, charged with the energy of attention, of consciousness itself, but it in no way excluded humor or light-heartedness. In fact, it included both.

I could not help but feel that not only was Marie the source of the guidelines that structured these remarkable proceedings, but also that her energy helped animate our listening and focus our remarks. I was keenly aware of her presence, and sometimes I scanned her face looking for clues about how she was responding to what all of us were saying—but most importantly, of course, to what I was saying. I found that my natural instinct, upon sketching out and then orally delivering my impressions of poems, was to tune into their sound and rhythm, which I then somewhat haltingly commented upon.

I had the sense that Marie was responding positively both to my observations and to the halting way, replete with disfluencies—the residue of the mild case of dyslexia with which I had been diagnosed as a child—in which they had been delivered.

Somehow, Marie and her reactions to my musings had become important, perhaps too important, to me. I certainly began to feel something like love and reverence for her. Somewhat embarrassingly, considering my age, she was becoming, I suppose, the image, or rather the embodiment, of a kind of idealized mother figure for me—a mother exacting, fiercely observant, and yet compassionate, quite unlike my own.

During the second section of each class, it was very obviously the teacher who was the center of attention. To begin with what might seem like a mere aside: Marie was a Catholic. I suspect, though she never talked about it, that she was in her own way a devout one. She was not only a Catholic but a member of that remarkable species, the Catholic intellectual, which perhaps accounted for the Jesuitical clarity and focused attentiveness with which she discussed both our poems and the poems that she brought to the class.

I began to notice, in her discussion of these poems, a tendency to shuttle from part to whole, whole to part. I realized that in listening to her I was hearing from a poet who read poems in much the same way that I do. Marie thought, in large part, abstractly, but always with a keen attention, as well, to concrete detail.

I cannot do justice to her remarkable poetry here, beyond making a few general observations. Marie was one of those rare poets who writes equally well, and with something like equal frequency, in free verse and in form. She tends to be regarded as a formal poet because her formal poems are remarkably deft and inventive. She has written not only a number of conspicuously superb sestinas but also abbreviated sestinas she called *tritenas*, a form of her own invention, whose stanzas are comprised of three lines instead of six, resulting in poems that are half as long as, and much punchier and pithier than, sestinas. She has written, as well, linked sonnet sequences in which the last line of the previous sonnet becomes the first line of the next. Often, but not always, both in her formal and in her free-verse poems, she cuts the rhythm of her poems slightly against the expected bias, undercutting what I suspect for her could have been too facile, too merely mellifluous cadences. The effect of some of these poems is akin to that of rubbing the nap of certain kinds of carpets against the grain, a procedure that sometimes reveals a deep strain or stain of intensified color. Like the poems of Gerard Manley Hopkins, one of her idols, Marie's poems are often "counter, original, spare, strange."

Some of Marie's more angular, free-verse poems in particular evince a mind that is always seriously at play. Many of these poems display a dazzling metaphysical wit. Others hint at subtle states of consciousness and feeling.

As a young woman, Marie received a master's degree from Columbia in seventeenth-century English poetry, so she came by her poetic wit honestly. Her canted, giddy, slightly off-balance poems, in which ideas are framed and reframed, all the while wedded with keen perceptions, are in no way derivative and have a jaunty music entirely her own.

Though Marie's poems reflect what I suspect is a deep spirituality, they often resist, even as they register, the oceanic pull of the mystical. She favors, often, a countervailing impulse toward a complex individuation, and so she has a respect for the individuated and the individual in the world that surrounds her, a world whose rich and delightful otherness is both accepted and celebrated.

It is difficult to pick any one representative work of a first-rate poet, particularly in the case of a poet like Marie, who wrote, as I have mentioned, poems of many different kinds. Her free-verse poems deploy what is perhaps the equivalent of complex jazz rhythms. Her more formal poems are classical, almost Mozartian.

I want something of the range of Marie's voice as a poet to be heard here, and so I will briefly address poems of both types. Of the first type is "Springing," which Marie chose as the title poem of her collection *Springing: New and Selected Poems.* The title of the poem, typically, is wittily polysemous, punning on Hopkins' heavily stressed "sprung rhythm," a version of which she deploys in the poem; on spring as the season of rejuvenation; and on her poetry's tendency to spring from one unexpected trope to another.

SPRINGING

In a skiff on a sunrisen lake we are watchers.

Swimming aimlessly is luxury just as walking
loudly up a shallow stream is.

As we lean over the deep well, we whisper.

Friends at hearths are drawn to the one warm air;
strangers meet on beaches drawn to the one wet sea.

What wd it be to be water, one body of water
(what water is is another mystery) (We are
water divided.) It wd be a self without walls,
with surface tension, specific gravity a local
exchange between bedrock and cloud of falling and rising,
rising to fall, falling to rise.

The poem, like many by Marie, conveys a sense of exhilaration and even wonder that is difficult to account for. Its initial brief stanzas, each comprised of one sentence, feel airy, full of space, almost weightless, unpredictable at every turn. Its final stanza grows denser, deliberately chancing the "surface tension," the "specific gravity" (another metaphysically witty pun) of its *almost* ungainly close.

"Springing," among other things, is clearly a love poem, one that plays with its central conceit that our bodies are mostly comprised of the primal element of water. Again like many of Marie's poems, it includes questions, implicit or explicit, wondering "what it would be to be water," "what water is," and what it would be to be "one body." Though lovers' bodies are "water divided" and thus necessarily individuated, they are also involved with, assimilated to, the cyclical transformations of water itself, moving from cloud to bedrock then back to cloud again, "rising to fall, falling to rise."

Ultimately, like Donne's "The Ecstasy," "Springing" enshrines the paradox of unity in duality, duality in unity. It avoids the pat, the neatly falsifying, while seeming all the while to hover in a space between disclosing itself and not disclosing itself. Many of Marie's poems seem somehow to guard their mysteries even as they gesture toward them.

As an example of Marie's work in a more formal mode, I will cite here a sestina that is a dialogue between the poet's older and younger selves—an updated version of the dramatized internal dialogues between, for example, one's perishable self and one's soul, which are a frequent feature of the metaphysical poetry of which Marie continued to be a keen student.

The sestina is a poem of six and a half stanzas. The six end words of the first stanza must be repeated in a prescribed order in subsequent stanzas, and all six must again be repeated in a final, abbreviated three-line stanza. Sestinas have become quite popular. They tend to be whimsical or humorous. One seldom feels that the intelligence or spirit of the form itself, particularly the peculiar force of the repeated words, is fully exploited in these poems. Marie's sestina is a rare exception.

If "Springing" feels like a sleek, modernist chair whose frame is made of polished, blonde wood, "For My Old Self, at Notre Dame" is like a darkly burnished armoire, an antique that at the same time has nothing of the fusty datedness of an antique. The poem is set in the cathedral of Notre Dame in Paris. Its epigraph, appropriately in Latin, long the liturgical language of the cathedral in which the poem is set, means "she is tossed but does not sink" and has, since the fourteenth century, been the unofficial motto of Paris. One more than suspects that this wittily deployed epigraph slyly serves here as Marie's motto for herself as well as for the many resilient women about whom she writes. Finally, Hopkins is never far from Marie's heart or ear, and so the epigraph may also be a kind of faint, far-fetched, perhaps unconscious allusion to Hopkins' "The Wreck of the Deutschland," a poem about a ship with a cargo of nuns that was tossed and alas *did* sink, though the souls of its passengers instead rose heavenward, consummating the promise of redemption.

I feel the need to mention here, as an aside, that I wrote this essay before the recent tragic fire at the cathedral. I thought of excising it, then thought better of it. Like people, poems change over the course of their lives as circumstances change. That this poem now cannot help but have a slightly less celebratory, more elegiac feel is not necessarily a loss and may be a gain. An elegiac strain, or to use Marie's words, an elegiac "grain" or "stain," was already implicit in the poem. Now it has become more pronounced, and so the poem has come to serve its reader in a slightly different way.

FOR MY OLD SELF, AT NOTRE-DAME

fluctuate nec mergitur

The dark madonna cut from a knot of wood
has robes whose folds make waves against the grain
and a touching face—noble in side view,
impish or childish seen head-on from above.
The wood has the rich stain of tannin, raised
to all-color luster by the steep of time.

The mouths of her shadows are pursed by time
to suck sun-lit memories from the wood.
Freezing damp and candle-smut have raised
her eyebrows into wings flung up by the grain,
caught in the light of bulbs plugged high above.
She stands alert, as if hailed, with breasts in view.

Outside of the jeweled river-ship, I view
a girl's back, walking off. Oh. Just in time
I shut up. She'd never hear me shout above
the tour guides and the ski-skate kids. How I would
have liked to see the face again, the grain
of beauty on her forehead, the chin raised

startled; her Who are you? wild, a question raised
by seeing me, an old woman, in plain view.
Time is a tree in me; in her it's a grain
ready to plant. I go back in, taking my time
leafy among stone trunks that soar in stone woods
where incense drifts, misty, lit pink from above.

She's headed for her hotel room then above
Cluny's garden. She'll sit there, feet raised,
notebook on her knee, to write. Maybe she would
have turned, known us both in a larger view
and caught my age in the freshness of its time.
She dreads clocks, she says. Such dry rot warps the grain.

They still say mass here. Wine and wheat grain
digest in flesh to words that float above
six kneeling women, a man dressed outside time,
and the dark madonna, her baby raised
dangerously high to pull in our view.
Magic dame, cut knot, your ancient wood

would reach back to teach her if it could. Spring rain.
Through it all I call to thank her, loud above
the joy she raised for me, this soft fall. Sweet time.

"...Robes whose folds make waves against the grain." How beautifully this first metaphor captures the movement of Marie's poetry itself! The poem does not merely enact a personal drama but also serves as a tribute to the Madonna, the divine mother, patron saint of all mothers and their offspring. The "Old Self" in the title of the poem is, of course, the poet's young self. The child is mother to the woman; the Madonna is the mother of both, and the generatrix of us all.

Finally, the poem reflects Marie's affinity for things French. As I have mentioned earlier, Marie was married to a French painter, spent much time in France, and helped to support her family by translating French books into English. Indeed, the sestina itself originated centuries ago in France.

In sum, the poem is a series of transparencies laid one over the other, each letting the others shine through. The use of the repeated end word "grain" suggests a tree whose variously scored rings are all luminously in view. It also, naturally, invokes the seed time of youth and the bread of the Eucharist through which the temporal touches the eternal.

As in all good sestinas, the poem's repeated end words are polyvalent, accruing and exploring multiple meanings as the poem progresses. As is appropriate for a poem that thematizes the relationship between an adult and and an earlier self, and that is set in a Gothic cathedral, intended to align time with eternity, the poem's key, its master end word, is *time* itself —"just in time / taking my time / in the freshness of time / outside time," and in the final two words of the poem, "sweet time." The word *time* tolls like a powerful but barely audible bell. The poem, though it strikes elegiac notes, is finally gently life-affirming, a congeries of multiple accords.

Marie's poems, whether free or formal, tend toward the celebratory. Though they fully acknowledge struggle, it is largely through the depiction of the valiant overcoming of it or, more rarely, of the valiant living with it. She, like Wallace Stevens, despite an awareness of the negative and the life-denying, and of the sometimes horrific situations, both personal and societal, in which we find ourselves, is a poet who says "yes" because of "a passion for yes that had never been broken."

And yet time, though sweet, also destroys. The poem provides a cogent example of how events in the circumambient world, not to mention in our own smaller worlds, affect our readings of poems. In a less spectacular way, poems are always transformed by their readers. Such readings are their only afterlife, renewing and revitalizing in the present what was written in the past. Sometimes, as is the case with Marie's poem on the cathedral, the imperative to regard a poem in a new way can be painful. One does not therefore expunge it from the record.

Ultimately, Marie's poetry is impossible to categorize. Her first book, *True Minds*, was published by Lawrence Ferlinghetti, whom she met, fortuitously, on a ship during a trans-Atlantic passage. The two became good friends. Ferlinghetti's City Lights Books, of course, was the publisher of choice of the Beats. *True Minds* was published in close temporal proximity to Ginsberg's "Howl." And yet Marie's poems, though they share a kind of iconoclasm, sound nothing like those of the Beats. They also, though often written in form, sound nothing like the formalist poems of those who were allied with what was then called New Criticism.

I recall having read an interview with Marie in which she laments the increasing lack of interest on the part of poets in exploring the rich resources of meter, syntax, and tone that writing in form can provide. At the same time, she expresses reservations about the work of the more doctrinaire among the poets of my generation who have dubbed themselves "New Formalists," whose forays into writing in form—whether in lyrics or what they call "The New Narrative"—too often, though with several exceptions, feel pallid, pinched, and constrained, like children who have learned too well to mind their manners.

I have written elsewhere, disparagingly, of what I consider the inept and dispiriting, too self-consciously avant-garde work of so-called L-A-N-G-U-A-G-E poets, who are under the delusion that their putatively politically radical work will have some kind of actual ameliorative social impact. Their work, at its worst, degenerates into a kind of entropic sprawl and abjures the imperatives of the pleasure principle, which seems to me to play a vital role in most poetry to which we feel drawn to return.

The poets of my generation who most interest me tend, like Marie, to work with something like equal facility in both form and free verse, and to erect no arbitrary barriers between them.

3.

When our classes had come to an end, my fellow classmates and I typically proceeded to the nearest subway station, whereas Marie proceeded in the opposite direction, toward Eighth Avenue, to catch a cab and head uptown to her apartment. It seemed to me somehow ungallant to leave Marie thus unaccompanied, and I resolved that at the end of the last class I would muster my courage and walk with her the half a block or so to Eighth Avenue. I did so, and I also plunged into the traffic to nab a cab for her. Afterward I realized that this whole exercise had been misguided. I think that the suggestion, inadvertently conveyed by me, that Marie somehow needed help in navigating the world, was rankling. Marie was nothing if not fiercely independent.

Once again, the following summer, I took Marie's advanced class. I immediately took note of a fellow student, a fiercely intelligent black woman who emanated a glowing, radiant energy, who tended to write quite long poems in which there was always a strong narrative element. Many of them are gritty accounts of the travails of race in America and other matters political and ethical. In the third and final section of the last class, she was one of the two poets whose work was to be intensively scrutinized. The poem she read was about a soldier who was in a coma after having been a victim of an IED in Iraq. The poem gave voice to some of his thoughts prior to the attack. It seemed to me that his musings indicated a startling lack of introspection about why he was in Iraq to begin with, and an almost complete naiveté with regard to matters political.

Something about this portrayal, as I perceived it, felt stereotypical and presumptuous. During the period in which we were all commenting upon the poem, rather than simply recounting my observations, I instead focussed on my reservations about it, my *judgement* of it. Almost immediately I recognized that I had abrogated the cardinal ground rule of the class. The moment felt strangely awkward, then passed. I sensed, or thought that I sensed, Marie's surprise and disappointment at my remarks.

During our walk to the subway, I apologized profusely to my fellow student for my breach of etiquette. She couldn't have been more gracious. She even said that she found my remarks insightful and helpful. Still, I couldn't help but feel troubled that I had chastised a black student for a poem, ironically, that I had faulted for being stereotypical. It was the inadvertence of the remark that particularly troubled me. I felt that I had publicly betrayed something in myself that I felt ashamed to betray, revealing an habitual unconsciousness that, to make matters worse, I might have preferred had remained unconscious.

I wished that it would in some way be possible for me to remain in touch with Marie after this second workshop ended, but I lacked the courage to make this wish known. I also felt that it would be wrong to make it known, to put her on the spot. And in fact, I had already made it known. After the class had ended the prior year, I had written Marie a long, ecstatic, perhaps too-intimate message via email, a kind of rash note about my experience of the class and implicitly about her. I received no response. I suspect that something in the tone of this electronic missive felt excessively needy, especially coming from a man of my age.

Marie had become a powerful presence in my life. I felt sad that I would likely never again see her.

At the very end of the last class, as I was leaving, Marie said to me, "You are a tricky one." I was unable to read her tone, which seemed matter-of-fact rather than either affectionate or censorious. These last words kept reverberating in my mind like a koan. I still do not know what she meant by them nor what feeling, if any, they were intended to convey. That Marie's last words to me were in the form of a cryptic utterance felt somehow appropriate. I was left not with the illusion of closure but with an open-ended question. Marie characteristically, as in her poems, had not fully disclosed herself; she had retained her measure of mystery.

4.

Attending Marie's class led me to muse about how poetry might best be taught not only to initiates in advanced poetry classes but to non-initiates of whatever age.

Again, the reading of poetry in particular is at least initially a form of listening. The quality of any response to a poem, including our value judgements about it, is to some degree commensurate with the quality and duration of the listening that has preceded it.

Most poets and much poetry exhibit a kind of resistance to being preemptively read critically, to being reductively paraphrased by an analytical intelligence that too often seeks to extract a stable meaning or meanings from a poem. This resistance should be respected. The intent of poets is not to be obscurantists but rather to ensure that their poems, by at first bypassing or overwhelming the operations of the analytic intellect, be read intuitively. Such a strategy does not, except in special cases, entirely bypass the intellect but rather insists that the intellect come into play *after* a poem has begun to be apprehended intuitively.

As a reader of poetry, I initially scan poems for their sound and for whatever as yet inchoate resonances of feeling they stir up in me; only later do I bring whatever analytic skills I possess to bear. It seems to me that the kind of order that I am suggesting—that one first responds to poetry intuitively and feelingly, and then rationally—is in effect the natural order of things. In a quite direct way, we respond to poems emotionally and kinesthetically before we respond to them intellectually.

One of the truly deadly things about the teaching of poetry to non-initiates of whatever age is that it cuts short what might be called "the intelligence of the heart." A student's initial experience of being stirred in some indefinable way by a poem, of being moved by it, or of being bored or threatened by it, or indifferent to it, or even hostile to it—before the student has had time even to breathe—is routinely bypassed. Teachers too often tend to go directly for the jugular, for the intelligence of the head, as a result of which students feel that if they cannot extract some prescribed nugget of meaning from a poem they simply *don't get* poetry and never will. And so the whole project is effectively scuttled even before it has begun. Many teachers, who themselves have little feeling for poetry except, sadly, as a result of their own miseducation, feel intimidated or nonplussed by it, and prefer not to teach it at all.

The general excuse given for the teaching of literature and poetry to impressionable young minds seems to be that it fosters the development of analytic skills. But surely there are more direct and effective ways of teaching such skills. This rationale, with respect to both poems and their students, constitutes a needless miscarriage of justice. Surely it would be more effective and humane simply, initially, to expose students to poetry, and thereafter to solicit their non-discursive, felt responses to it, as the first step in a process by which, hopefully, the study of poetry will help the student to explore, cultivate, and begin to trust his or her own felt intuition in navigating not only poems but the obstacle course of the so-called real world. It seems to me that the cultivating of such intuition is primarily what poetry has to teach us.

Only after a long latency period should the intellectual analysis of poems, or perhaps rather, the close observation of poems and of the myriad ways in which they either do or do not work, be introduced. Even here, the emphasis on how poems work (in the spirit of William James, and of the native strain of pragmatism endorsed by his many successors) rather than on the obsessive target practice involved in determining what they may or may not mean, should be paramount. Questions regarding meaning and the lack of it will quite naturally arise as a byproduct of such observations.

One would hope that teachers of poetry feel some love for it. This, of course, is an unrealistic expectation. It is perhaps slightly less unrealistic to hope that they teach with the intention, like Taoist sages, of getting out of the way, thus allowing at least a few interested students to discover, through felt intuition, poetry's sometimes urgent wish to address them. As a result of listening to such urgent addresses, one would hope what begins for the student as a sometimes difficult voyage of discovery leads to a kind of inexhaustible process of self-discovery, a process with which Marie clearly, for all her wisdom and for all her years, still remained passionately and vitally engaged.

2. William Maxwell

When I was a child and thereafter, William and Emily Maxwell were close friends of my parents. He was a novelist and a long-time editor of *The New Yorker;* she was a painter and a devoted wife who happened to be extraordinarily beautiful. There was something slightly unreadable, a sense that much was held in reserve, about both of them. While I was growing up, Bill was not nearly as well known, or indeed as almost famous, as he has since become.

Bill's presence did not register particularly strongly on me as a child. There was something slightly recessive and unforthcoming about it, qualities that children are unlikely to find endearing. And yet my mother had a profound, often expressed, admiration for writers, including for Bill, about whom she often spoke, and so, of course, I was subliminally encouraged to regard him as both exceptional and exemplary.

After I was dispatched to boarding school at the age of twelve, I was home only during the summer months, during which my family lived in a house on Long Island Sound rather than New York City. No dinner parties occurred there, and Bill and Emily thus receded from my view. In subsequent years, I seldom even briefly saw either of them.

Then matters quite suddenly changed. In my early forties, after some daunting travails, including long periods of depression, I was living, for the first time since my childhood, in New York City. By that time, I had read most of Bill's novels, and confess that, although I admired, with some reservations, all of them, I found *The Folded Leaf* in particular extraordinarily moving. It seemed to me a masterpiece, if perhaps a minor one. But minor masterpieces are almost as rare as full-fledged ones and deserve their full measure of respect.

By this time, in the early nineties, Bill was becoming increasingly well known. All of his novels had been reprinted by Vintage Books, and they were garnering renewed and mostly reverent attention. There had always been a cenacle, a circle of admirers around Bill and Emily, who had felt that Bill's fiction had been scandalously under-appreciated. They would continue to feel so even as Bill's reputation continued to grow, culminating with the publication of his complete works in two volumes by the Library of America.

In the many years subsequent to my childhood encounters with Bill, I had become a poet, if for a long time an unpublished one. After completing graduate school, I lived for well over a decade in the ashrams of a spiritual preceptor in India and in upstate New York. During these years, and for a time thereafter, I had made only cursory attempts to disseminate my work, which can be something like a full-time job.

Around 1997 or so, my mother mentioned to Bill that I was a poet, and that I had written several unpublished books, at which point Bill told my mother, with extraordinary generosity, that I should call him, that I should have tea with him at his apartment, and that I should bring one of my manuscripts with me. The call was made, and the date to have tea at Bill and Emily's apartment on York Avenue was duly arranged. On the one hand, I was appalled by my mother's uncharacteristic and unsolicited intervention; on the other, I was grateful for it.

Hence I found myself, on one mid-afternoon in midsummer, walking around and around a city block on the far East Side of Manhattan—"over by the river," to steal the title of one of Bill's most celebrated short stories. As usual, I had arrived at my destination early. The meeting that I had been anticipating for three weeks with mounting excitement and some anxiety was about to occur.

I should confess that I read relatively little fiction and feared that I would appear to be an ignoramus on the subject—which I, in fact to some degree, was and am. I had thought a lot about my upcoming encounter with Bill and finally decided on an opening gambit. I would tell Bill that his fiction reminded me a great deal of that of Willa Cather, particularly of *My Antonia* and of *O Pioneers*. As indeed it did. Both Bill and Cather hailed from the Midwest; both wrote of ordinary people in graceful prose that evinced a clear affection for their characters. Their writing had in common an elegant simplicity and a persistent, understated, almost subliminal but always keen and unerring orchestration of prose rhythm.

My heart racing, I rang the doorbell of Bill's apartment. He opened it and ushered me into a living room where tea had been prepared and laid out. Emily briefly emerged to greet me, then returned to her painting studio. The two of us were to be left alone. I handed Bill my manuscript apologetically, and he said that he looked forward to reading it.

Almost immediately I made my aforementioned opening gambit, telling him that his fiction reminded me of Willa Cather's. Bill lit up. It turned out that Cather was an author with whom he felt a considerable affinity and whose writing at its best, as in the two novels I mentioned, he deeply admired. It was a kind of hunch or intuition that had led me to making what I am too cynically calling a gambit. Again, such intuition, which can be honed in part through reading and writing poetry, is not without its applications in the real world.

In any event, my opening foray worked, completely dissipating my anxiety, and for the rest of our conversation, Bill and I were on the same wavelength—or at least I felt that we were. I have no doubt, too, that Bill was doing his best to put me at ease.

The rest of the afternoon unfolded as though I had been in a kind of benevolent dream or trance. For two hours, our talk was uninterrupted. Then Emily emerged from her studio, which seemed an elegant cue that it was time for this particular entranced interlude to end. In retrospect, it is as though my time with Bill was bracketed by golden parentheses, a kind of reprieve from the vicissitudes and exigencies of the so-called real world.

The first of my teas with Bill occurred when he was eighty-six or eighty-seven, almost exactly the same age as Marie when I had providentially encountered her. Thereafter he would invite me over for tea several times a year. I suppose I saw him eight or nine times before both he and Emily became gravely ill. These talks, taken together, seemed an unbroken continuum. Each of our meetings commenced as though our prior meeting had been interrupted just a moment before. We indeed, during these meetings, seemed to be intuitive readers of each other as well empathically intuitive listeners. At the same time, I worried there was a slight imbalance, that perhaps I gained more from these meetings than did he. But this talk of relative gain is probably misplaced. Our experiences together could not be tallied as though upon some ledger. They were a gift while they lasted.

During our meetings, the subject of the manuscript of poetry that I had given Bill did not arise. At first, of course, I was disappointed. But before long I either completely forgot about this omission or didn't care. Or perhaps I did care and was in denial about it.

When we talked briefly about poetry, Bill mentioned his love of Yeats, which seemed unexceptionable, but in particular of his affection for the Edwardian poet, A. E. Housman, the author of *A Shropshire Lad*. Housman was a fine minor poet about whom I was pleased to be reminded. He was a classics scholar whose life's work, apart from the occasional writing of poems, was to make fastidious corrections to and emendations of classical texts. He is regarded to this day not merely as a good but as a great scholar, and some of his versions of Latin poems remain definitive. Housman was passionate about this work, which required patience, tact, and a highly refined intelligence. His justifiably high regard for his own scholarly work was matched only by his scorn and disdain for that of most of his predecessors and of all of his peers.

Bill, too, had a kind of tough and flinty side. I suspected that he, like me, was more of an immovable object than an irresistible force. He was happily and unapologetically sedentary and preferred being in his apartment to obligatory social forays into the world at at large. He especially disliked the banal palaver at cocktail parties. To some in such settings, Bill seemed diffident and opaque. It was this quality that had most struck me as a child. Clearly he felt under no obligation to be interesting, least of all to those who did not interest him. My mother told me at some point that, although he did his best to hide it, Bill did not suffer fools gladly. My brother-in-law, who is a brilliant designer and an astute judge of character, told me, after first meeting him, "I wouldn't want to get on his wrong side."

Since his days as an undergraduate, Housman had been deeply and hopelessly in love with his close friend Moses Jackson, who was an Olympic caliber runner. After their time together at Oxford, the two worked in the same patent office and shared a flat. After several years, Jackson abruptly moved out, some suspect as a result of Housman professing, or in my view more likely discreetly hinting at, the nature of his feelings to Jackson. Several years later, when Jackson married, he did not invite Housman to the wedding. Not long thereafter Jackson died. Housman was devastated. It was a blow from which he never fully recovered.

"A Shropshire Lad" is an evocation of a bygone era—or perhaps more properly, of an idealized era that never was. Set in in an imaginary county in rural England, the preoccupations of Housman's poems are similar to those of Thomas Hardy. Man is cast adrift in a universe governed by no deity. Nature, however alluring, is indifferent to him. The one incontrovertible fact is the inevitable passage of time that leads to death.

Housman's poetry expresses feeling simply and directly, often in economical quatrains. It found more favor initially in the United States than in England and was particularity attractive to younger readers. The high tide of Housman's reputation was reached in the 1920s, which coincided with Bill's youth and with the era in which a number of his novels, including *The Folded Leaf*, are set. Hence, perhaps, Bill's surprising enthusiasm for Housman. Housman's reputation began to ebb in the early 1930s, and it has been in decline ever since. His poems' apparent lack of irony and their easy amenability to paraphrase made them anathema to New Critics who reigned supreme in the middle decades of the last century. And yet these very qualities are also what gives Housman's poems their peculiar charm. As a scholar, he was a master, in particular, of the Latin love elegy. The best of his poems have a kind of burnished elegiac glow, which Maxwell too, particularly in *The Folded Leaf* but also in earlier novels that are set in his childhood, powerfully evokes.

A number of Housman's poems are brief pastoral elegies for youths who have had both the good and the bad fortune to die early, in the prime of their beauty. One such poem is "To An Athlete Dying Young," which, like a Pindaric ode, is a celebration of the prowess of the athlete. Such prowess, as Housman recognized, is destined to quickly fade, and so death becomes a kind of boon:

> ...
> Now you will not swell the rout
> Of lads that wore their honours out,
> Runners whom renown outran
> And the name died before the man.
>
> So set, before its echoes fade,
> The fleet foot on the sill of shade,
> And hold to the low lintel up
> The still-defended challenge-cup
>
> And round that early-laurelled head
> Will flock to gaze the strengthless dead,
> And find unwithered on its curls
> The garland briefer than a girl's.

There is much that is oddly congruent between Housman's and Bill's life and work. Bill's legendary career at *The New Yorker* as the masterful editor of a number of extraordinary writers seems to me to parallel Housman's long career as a master emender of classical works. Both brought devotion, passion, and a fastidious eye to their work. For a long time, Bill was known primarily as an editor, not for his novels and short stories.

The central event in Bill's life was the sudden loss of his mother when he was ten. Partly as a result of this trauma, Bill, like Housman, had a somewhat dark, fatalistic view of the world. He, too, was an atheist, and literature became his secular religion.

The Folded Leaf, my favorite of Bill's books, which will be my main subject here, is one of Bill's many tales of loss. It is the story of the relationship between two boys that spans their last years of high school through the first year they spend together at college. One of the boys, Lymie Peters, is sensitive, introspective, bookish, and bright. He is also small and flat-chested. The other, Spud Latham, at first seems Lymie's opposite. He is an athlete who is more concerned with boxing than with books. He is introduced in the novel's first chapter, a scene in which a number of boys are playing water polo. All are stark naked, which affords Maxwell the opportunity to describe Spud's body in loving detail as both perfectly proportioned and unerringly graceful. Spud rescues Lymie from a gaggle of boys who are holding him underwater. As a result the two boys become unlikely friends.

The central ritual of the novel takes place in the gym where Spud is training to be a boxer. Every day Lymie joins him there. His somewhat menial task is to hand Spud his boxing gloves, to tie their laces when he puts them on, and then to wait around until the workout is over, whereupon he unties the laces, and then has to wait still more until Spud emerges naked from the shower and dresses. This daily ritual is in some sense one of worship. Lymie is the worshipper, and Spud the worshipped. At the outset of the novel, Spud has the grace simply to accept Lymie's devotion unquestioningly.

Early on in his and Lymie's freshman year in college, Spud and a girl named Sally fall in love. Sally is an almost entirely sympathetic character and becomes deeply fond of Lymie, who remains Spud's acolyte. Lymie becomes a kind of ubiquitous third wheel in their relationship. Sally's devotion to Lymie is genuine. They share something that is crucial to them. Both, after all, are deeply in love with Spud.

The central tragedy of the novel is the failure of the characters to read each other. Though on the one hand, they are the closest of friends, on the other, each fails at crucial moments to intuit what the other is feeling, leading to the kind of tragic consequences that such misreadings sometimes entail. Spud, though no intellectual, is no less sensitive than Lymie. His misreading of what Lymie and later his girlfriend are feeling for each other, at first a mere inkling of suspicion, leads him to contemplate leaving the room in a boardinghouse that he shares with Lymie and moving into a fraternity house. He hopes to be dissuaded by either Lymie or Sally as a proof of their affection for him. Neither voices any objection. Lymie, who is devastated by the thought of Spud's impending move, nevertheless, fearful of revealing his feelings, holds his tongue. Sally, though baffled, sees no compelling reason to voice any objection. As a result, hurt by their silence, Spud, overriding his own feelings, joins a fraternity that he has no wish to join, a misguided act that ratifies his unfounded suspicions and eventually leads to a rupture between him and his erstwhile friend.

There is a great deal in this moving novel to which I am unable, in a brief paraphrase, to do justice. At any rate, why should first-rate prose be amenable to paraphrase any more than is first-rate poetry? I am racing toward the novel's extraordinary final chapters, where I intend to tarry slightly longer.

Spud, who is jealous of the qualities in Lymie that he lacks, eventually becomes convinced that Sally and Lymie are secretly in love with each other. In his own way, again, Spud is as sensitive, fragile, and vulnerable as Lymie.

In a powerful sequence of scenes toward the end of the novel, Spud is a competitor in the Golden Gloves boxing tournament in Chicago. He is triumphant in the early rounds, although he slowly, by repeated blows, develops a gash on his forehead. In what should have been his penultimate match, Spud, venting the anger he feels toward Lymie and Sally, hits his opponent while he is down and so is disqualified.

The stress on Spud's suffering body, the pain and distress that it undergoes, is powerfully emphasized by Maxwell—as is the pain of Sally and Lymie in seeing the perfect body that both worship being desecrated. What should have been a moment of athletic glory and triumph for Spud, the equivalent of the triumph of the laurel-crowned young athlete in Housman's poem, or of the victorious athletes whom Pindar celebrates in his odes, becomes something else entirely.

Lymie has made what turns out to be the terrible mistake of buying Sally, just before they attend Spud's last bout, a bouquet of violets to affix to her blouse. Spud's suspicion that Lymie and Sally are in fact in love with each other hardens into a kind of certainty. Thereafter, Spud continues to allow Lymie to perform his usual ritual tasks at the gym but refuses to speak to him. Lymie hears of the jealousy and rage that Spud now feels for him and late one night goes to Spud's room and desperately tries to set the record straight, but Spud does not believe him. Lymie returns home and unsuccessfully attempts to commit suicide by slashing his wrists and neck with a straight razor.

After he has sufficiently recovered, Lymie receives two key visits in his hospital room. One is from Spud, who finally, in effect, gets the message and for the first time understands the nature and intensity of Lymie's love for and devotion to him.

> Spud came and sat on the edge of the bed. Neither he nor Lymie spoke. They looked at each other with complete knowledge at last, with full awareness of what they had meant to each other and of all that had ever passed between them. After a moment Spud leaned forward slowly and kissed Lymie on the mouth. He had never done this before and he was never moved to do it again.

The second visit is from Lymie's father, who expresses his hurt feelings and love, and makes himself vulnerable to Lymie by asking his son why he had not left a note that would have mitigated the guilt he would have felt had Lymie's suicide attempt been successful. Lymie simply replies that it hadn't occurred to him to do so. This response deeply wounds Lymie's father.

> He simply spoke the truth, but for a long time afterwards, for nearly a year, Mr. Peters held it against him. With that one remark the distance which had always been between them stretched out and became a vast tract, a desert country.

In the passage that follows, which is chapter 58, Maxwell metaphorically evokes this desert country of the heart and soul. It is an astonishingly beautiful, utterly surprising, and luminous piece of writing. Nothing else in Maxwell's writing matches its power. Here, I sense, he draws closest to the essential truth of his experience. The chapter begins:

> In desert country the air is never still. You raise your eyes and see a windmill a hundred yards away, revolving in the sunlight, without any apparent beginning and for years to come without any end. It may seem to slow up and stop but that is only because it is getting ready to go round and round again, faster and faster, night and day, week in and week out. The end that is followed by a beginning is neither end nor beginning. Whatever is alive must be continuous. There is no life that doesn't go on and on, even the life that is in water and in stones.

This continuum that neither stops nor starts, that in a sense has no real past or future, is a dimension of experience and of reality that merely and simply proceeds apart from, and is indifferent to, whatever vicissitudes, whether joys or sorrows, we may experience. Maxwell is evoking here, I think, something close to Housman's experience of nature as indifferent to man. And yet man too is a part of this continuum, is by no means entirely divorced from it, a fact that is revealed by his quotidian, his common, his day-to-day, experience.

> Listen and you hear children's voices, a dog's soft, padded steps, a man hammering, a man sharpening a scythe. Each of them is repeated, the same sound, stopping and starting like a windmill.

Here, importantly, yet again, it is listening through which we can tune into this continuous dimension of the world and our experience of it. I recall when I was living in a fourth-story, walk-up apartment in Brooklyn, after having long lived away from New York, listening to the different densities and distances of a vast variety of sounds that passed though my open window. Allowing myself to get lost in these sounds, I think I sensed something of the continuum of which Maxwell is writing. Significantly, again, it is particularly listening that grants us this experience: "Listen and you hear..."

What follows is the odd, seemingly obvious observation that we often need all of our senses, particularly vision and hearing, to apprehend certain aspects of reality, which, were one or the other lacking, would remain completely inaccessible to us. This passage culminates with the rhetorical statement: "But who is not, in one way or another, for large stretches of time, blind or deaf or both?" Maxwell then mentions the failure of Mrs. Forbes, the benignly maternal proprietress of the boarding house in which Lymie lives, to grasp an essential reality when Lymie's father passes in front of her window.

> She...failed to perceive that for the first time in many years he had tried to speak from his heart and had failed... All that Mrs. Forbes saw was a man getting old and heavy before his time.

The failure to listen and truly hear, the failure to watch and truly see, become metaphors for our failure, too often, to apprehend in any way the inner life of others. Some are particularly fated, it seems, never to be really seen or heard, never to be adequately understood, always to remain solitary, to remain in the desert. Lymie, as it turns out, is one of these people:

> The desert is the natural dwelling place not only of Arabs and Indians but also of people who can't speak when they want to and of those others who, like Lymie Peters, have nothing more to say, people who have stopped justifying and explaining, stopped trying to account for themselves or their actions, stopped hoping that someone will come along and love them and so make sense out of their lives.

This whole passage casts a different light on Spud's visit with Lymie. Initially, I think, we are relieved that Spud has gotten the message, and we are touched by the kiss that Spud bestows on Lymie. But now we realize that no further kiss will be forthcoming, and that once the nature of their relationship has been laid bare, there is "nothing more to say," and that it is essentially over. Certainly Lymie cannot continue to be the third rail in the relationship between Spud and Sally. Their destiny is to be with each other. Lymie is to remain alone in the desert, which at first seems to have compensatory gains, including a heightened ability first to see, then to hear:

There are things in the desert which aren't to be found anywhere else. You can see a hundred miles in every direction, when you step out of your front door, and at night the stars are even brighter than they are at sea. If you cannot find indoors what you should find, then go to the window and look at the mountains, revealed after two days of uncertainty, of no future beyond the foothills which lie in a circle around the town. If it is not actually cold, if you aren't obliged to hug the fire, then go outside, by all means, even though the air is nervous, and you hear wind in the poplars, a train, a school bell, a fly—all sounds building toward something which may not be good.

The wind in the poplars, the train, the school bell, the fly, like the children's voices, the dog's steps, and the sound of the hammer and the scythe mentioned earlier in the chapter, all are part of the continuum of which, as previously mentioned, we are a part, but which is also in some way indifferent to us, a continuum to which one can attune oneself by a kind of listening. Only this time the continuum is perhaps not merely indifferent, but "building toward something which may not be good."

As for the foothills that surround the town, perhaps they have been obscured for two days by the weather, resulting in two days of uncertainty. Or perhaps the uncertainty is caused by something else, but ultimately there is "no future beyond [them]," nor even in the majestically rising mountains themselves, just as for Lymie, now that his relationship with Spud and Sally is drawing toward its inevitable close, no viable future presents itself.

The last passage in Maxwell's revised version of *The Folded Leaf* leaves us with a vision of Lymie, Sally, and Spud together again perhaps for one last time, playing a childish game on Lymie's hospital bed. But they are no longer children. Sally and Spud will proceed into the future together. Lymie, again, must return to the desert.

The book, in short, seems to me unbearably sad, and this unbearable sadness, and the desert country with which *The Folded Leaf* ends, are at the heart of Bill's literary country. It was first caused by the sudden death of Bill's mother when he was ten, a blow from which he never fully recovered, and this sudden and irrevocable loss is referred to, to one degree or another, in all of his novels with the exception of *The Chateau*. The rest of Bill's novels keep obsessively returning to the times and places of his childhood and youth. It is commonplace to say of those who have suffered extreme trauma that their emotional development is arrested at the time when the trauma occurred. Though Bill's writing supports such a presumption, his life, in which one senses he confronted and overcame much, and continued to grow as a person, does not.

It is well known, because Bill has made it known, that he himself attempted to commit suicide at the age of nineteen, one presumes as a result of a relationship similar to that which is described in *The Folded Leaf*, one which entailed yet another irreparable loss. Bill claimed that the book had "all of his youth in it."

My reaction to Bill's novel was intensified by the fact that in my own youth, I had had an experience very close to that depicted in *The Folded Leaf*. During my junior and senior years at the boarding school I attended, I was deeply in love with my roommate. He, too, was physically beautiful, and I imagined myself at the time as anything but. Of course, I could not avoid watching him dress and undress.

Just as I was suffering, I knew that he, too, was suffering, but I did not know why. I desperately wanted to divulge my feelings but could not imagine how the two of us could live together after such a revelation. It was only after we had graduated, when it was too late, when the whole thing was over, that I wrote him of my feelings, and that he in reply wrote me of what it was that had been causing his own suffering.

I had not even managed to muster up, like Lymie, the courage to express my devotion. These two final years of high school, entailing a kind of enforced silence, were devastating for me. As a result of this experience, I felt dead inside, as though I had been deposited in some place even more hopeless than Bill's desert country. I sleep-walked through my first year in college and then suffered a devastating suicidal depression from which I eventually emerged.

It seemed utterly clear to me, after reading *The Folded Leaf*, that it is a novel about a certain kind of homosexual love, and that it was therefore the first, and in my view the most compelling, gay, postwar novel. And yet even in our era of queer theory, for some reason this fundamental thrust of the book has never been fully, straightforwardly acknowledged. Those who write about it often perform little minuets, suggesting that the book's depictions of physical intimacy certainly have something striking about them, something perhaps homoerotic, while at the same time never quite addressing the unbearable emotional intensity of the novel. So we have a coming-of-age story with a few homoerotic references, not a novel that is, whatever else it is, painfully frank. And so Bill's finest novel, almost as though its subject has been suppressed, has never assumed its proper, preeminent position in relation to his other books. What seems to me an obfuscation of *The Folded Leaf* has resulted in *So Long, See You Tomorrow*, an elegantly written, affecting, yet slightly desiccated novella, being widely regarded as Bill's finest work.

During my quietly lovely and transporting teas with Bill, I assumed, in part from reading *The Folded Leaf*, that we were both gay, an understanding on my part that would have been absurd and completely pointless to express and that had no bearing on the intimacy of our encounters. An important caveat: I am writing here of *my* experience of Bill. I claim no special insight into Bill's experience of himself. Indeed, as I have indicated, there was something mysterious about Bill, mysterious and complex. The imagination is the enemy of the fixed and the categorical, the ally of the dynamic. Sexual identity, as the generation now coming of age reminds us, is for many part of a continuum. It is not fixed, but fluid. I don't think that gayness is for most gay people the preeminent, defining characteristic of either their personalities or their lives. But surely it is an important one.

Here I fear I am transgressing, saying what might have been better left unsaid. It is entirely possible that I have projected my own high school experience and my own experience of myself as gay, not only upon *The Folded Leaf* but upon Bill himself. After all, it was Bill who repeatedly insisted that the novel is about romantic love of all kinds, not about sex, a judgement that likely leads to some of the critical minuets described above, and that seems to me to be belied by the remarkable amount of attention paid to Spud's naked body throughout the novel.

At some point, however, I discovered that Bill had said that the event in his life that resulted in his suicide attempt was a betrayal by a friend who had slept with Bill's girlfriend. In other words, it is possible that what seems to have been a heterosexual scenario became, by the alchemy of the imagination, a gay one.

Nevertheless, were I a betting man, which I am not, I would bet that Bill had struggled with his sexual identity during an earlier, largely unchronicled phase of his life.

Bill once remarked that during William Shawn's regime as editor-in-chief of *The New Yorker*, he had had to follow marching orders and to either delete or mitigate the "lust" that had started to crop up in John Cheever's late work, some instances of which, as in his fine and courageous novella *Falconer*, were homosexual lust. John Updike, in the meantime—surely then, and even still, among the most overrated of novelists, of whom it could be said, in the words of Queen Gertrude's address to Hamlet's players, "more matter with less art"—had written *Couples*, a book that was controversial for its many graphic, and it seemed to me clinical and entirely unsexy, depictions of sex. It appeared that lust, heterosexual lust, was not considered out of bounds for him; or perhaps the stories he chose to submit to *The New Yorker* were free of it.

Regardless, all of this genteel, fastidious repression was taking place within the context of the sexual revolution of the late-sixties to the mid-seventies. The kind of fiction *The New Yorker* published came to be seen by some as insular, parochial, willfully oblivious, cut off from the exigencies of the political, and as worshipping at the altar of a certain kind of fine writing in which obeisance to the immaculate sentence was paramount. Cheever, accepting a prestigious award while wasting away from cancer, remarked that there "is nothing as invincible as a page of good prose." Bill often remarked that the one thing that made him uncomfortable with death was that he would no longer be able to read Tolstoy. Again, this kind of elevating of a page of good prose into a kind of secular religion feels to me not only parochial but somehow affected, unreal, distorted by a too-limited perspective.

While what Shawn called *lust* can be edited out of fiction, sex cannot not so easily edited out of life. Of course, most of Bill's work centered around his childhood, and so the issue of lust, which might equally fittingly, in some cases, be called sexual love, simply does not arise. Somehow, nonetheless, and particularly in some of his stories that have adult protagonists, I feel that the absence of the erotic and its energies, even, oddly, the lack of a sense of its sublimated energy beneath the surface of his work, accounts for a kind enervation that I sometimes feel in Bill's never less than scrupulously calibrated prose.

Of course, eros sometimes expresses itself most powerfully by *not* being explicitly acknowledged, by remaining subliminal, implicit. I am not speaking only of homo- or heterosexual eroticism but also of the erotic more widely construed as a kind of vitality and life force. But this kind of intense subliminal repression and the erotic suggestiveness it entails does not seem to me, with the notable exception of *The Folded Leaf*, to be a feature of much of Bill's work. The world of his fiction can feel oddly circumscribed. It is part of its charm, but it is also, I think, a limitation. George Bernard Shaw once remarked that vulgarity is an essential part of any great writer's repertoire. It was not a part of Bill's.

While writing *The Folded Leaf*, Bill was a client of the well-known psychoanalyst Theodore Reik, who made it be known that he thought, for Bill's own well-being, that his book needed to have a more generative, more life-embracing, more optimistic ending—in effect, reflecting the psychoanalytic prejudices of the time, a less gay ending. And so Bill added to the book its 62nd and final chapter, in which somehow Lymie's scars, both physical and emotional, have been miraculously healed; in which, in a symbolic passage that is as trite as the passage about the desert is transcendent, Lymie plants flowers in a forest; and in which, finally, he happily dons a turtleneck shirt to hide his scars and agrees to go out on a date with a girl named Hope. The passage is such an embarrassment that Bill removed it in the first Vintage reprinting of the book, but he later inexplicably allowed it to creep back into subsequent editions.

There is, however, an irony in all of this. Reik's project of leading Bill toward a less lonely and pessimistic life and toward a more generative one, an attempt to lead Bill, in effect, out of the desert, though it had unfortunate repercussions for his finest novel, may well have led him to intently pursue, upon meeting her, and to insist upon marrying Emily Noyes, an extraordinarily beautiful and talented young woman thirteen years his junior.

There were long gaps between the publication of *The Folded Leaf, Time Will Darken It*, and *The Chateau*, Bill's first and only novel about an adult relationship. The fifteen or so years between Bill's entry into adulthood and his marriage to Emily were never written about, nor even, as I recall, spoken about. I suspect that they were for Bill quite painful years spent in the desert. It is possible that that desert was simply the landscape bequeathed to him by the death of his mother. Bill's job at *The New Yorker* and his marriage to Emily all lead to his exodus from that desert as, of course, did Bill's own determination and willpower. And yet I think, without question, he always carried the desert within him. That inaccessible, lonely, in some sense secret and sealed-off space made him more interesting, more mysterious, more complex, more human than some of Bill's well-intentioned hagiographers have made him out to be.

Bill and Emily's marriage was legendary. It seems to have been, and I think was, one of those deep, mysterious relationships that led to a continued flowering of the lives of both parties.

When we were children, my sisters and I were allowed to wander for ten or fifteen minutes among the couples that assembled for our parents' aforementioned not-infrequent dinner parties. In a relatively large numbers of these marriages, the husbands were gay. Though we tended to be monopolized by more gregarious couples, I remember being particularly struck, if usually from afar, by Bill and Emily, perhaps because of her beauty, and also perhaps because I felt, as a child, something of their mysterious, self-sufficient closeness.

Eventually Bill and Emily became too ill for my visits to continue. Then what seemed to me a remarkable coincidence occurred. For many years after having discovered my vocation as a poet while in college, I lived, as briefly noted above, in the ashrams of a guru, or spiritual preceptor, in India and in upstate New York. During the time of my meetings with Bill, I was no longer living in the ashram, which was now run my first preceptor's designated successor, a powerful woman who had in turn become my spiritual teacher. A friend of mine who was her secretary sometimes suggested books for her to read. My friend had coincidently found an old copy of Bill's book *The Old Man and the Railroad Crossing* in a bookcase at her family's apartment. The book contains a number of brief stories that Bill had invented and read to his children at bedtime. Some instinct led my friend to bring it to my teacher who, as it turned out, was enraptured by it. She, too, read from it every night before bedtime. It was because my teacher had such an unprecedentedly strong reaction to the book that my friend mentioned it to me. She wanted to know if I knew anything about the author. I replied that I knew a great deal about him and mentioned that both Bill and his wife were dying. I told her something about Emily as well, including the fact that she was a talented and respected painter.

The following day, I received a phone call from my friend, who had recounted our conversation to our teacher. She had apparently written a note to Bill and Emily and wished that I relay it to them, along with two beautiful silk scarves. These items were forthwith dispatched to me from my teacher's ashram in upstate New York by courier. And so I found myself, in turn, dialing the number of Bill and Emily's household. Their daughter Kate answered the phone, and I asked her if would it be alright for me to drop off the note and scarves downstairs with a doorman. Kate suggested that I should bring the note to her parents' apartment and should spend an afternoon there.

And so I once again found myself ringing the Maxwells' doorbell and was met not by Kate but by her sister Brooke, who clearly had no idea who I was, nor why she should be admitting me into the inner sanctum. After a few fumbling remarks on my part, she motioned me into the apartment. I discovered quite a lively scene. At any given time, several writers who were among Bill's cenacle, the charmed circle of almost worshipful admirers who had come to surround Emily and Bill, were in attendance. So many people filled the same living room in which Bill and I had had our charmed meetings! All seemed to know each other. None knew me. I felt like an interloper. At the same time, I felt like announcing that I had known Bill and Emily since the age of three, thus establishing my *bona fides*. Fortunately, the fine novelist Annabel Davis-Goff (whose vivid memoir of her Anglo-Irish upbringing, *Walled Gardens,* has much in common with Bill's work) noticed my discomfort and came to my rescue. We had a warm and lively conversation.

Those in Bill's inner circle were mostly, like Bill, acolytes of literature as a kind of secular religion for whom Bill was a patron saint. Great artists tend not to be saints. I felt, again, that a worshipful attitude toward Bill was actually a disservice to him, bypassing his mysterious complexity as a character as well as the desert places which he still carried within him.

At some point we were briefly admitted, in two shifts, into Emily's bedroom. I was utterly shocked by how completely wasted her body was. At the same time, she was surrounded by a kind of radiant, numinous glow at the center of which were her fully alert eyes. For the first time, I *almost* experienced someone's luminous aura. Emily simply wanted to acknowledge us, to direct a nod and a smile toward each of us. I felt very much as though I were receiving a blessing. I found myself wishing that I had spent more time with her, wishing that I had asked, for example, to visit her studio and to see some of her work. Shortly after our visits to her bedroom, she made it known that the transition that she and her husband were going through should be considered a cause for celebration. She made sure that someone picked up a cache of delicious pastries that she had ordered for all in attendance to enjoy.

My friend from the ashram had read my teacher's letter to Bill and Emily to me over the phone, so I knew what was included in it. The letter was essentially a note of thanks. Acknowledging both Bill and Emily's work as artists, it expressed a deep appreciation of their selfless practice of their vocations, and for the particular and unique insights that had brought joy to many and which in the process had uplifted them.

Though there was no mention in it of anything overtly spiritual, I felt a bit abashed at relaying this letter to Bill, whom I knew to be an atheist. And yet at the very least it could do no harm, and I suspected that he would likely accept it simply as a welcome appreciation from a source so unlikely as to delight him. I suspected, without knowing it, that Emily had a rich spiritual life. When Kate called me a few days later, she reported that Emily wanted me to know that she had found the scarf beautiful, and that she had been touched by the fact that my teacher had acknowledged her as an artist on an equal footing with her husband. A few days later Emily died, and a week after that Bill, too, was gone.

I experienced the chance to visit Bill and Emily's apartment one last time as a kind of compound blessing, both from my spiritual teacher and from Bill and Emily themselves. All, of course, remarked upon how appropriate, fortuitous, and coincidentally wonderful it was that Bill and Emily had died within a week of each other. I remember thinking that it was perhaps not so fortunate for their daughters.

About a month later, on a beautiful summer day, I attended Bill and Emily's memorial service at Saint John the Divine, the great, unfinished Episcopal Cathedral in the upper West Side of Manhattan. Its cavernous space was packed. Bill and Emily indeed had touched many. I felt a bit abashed and humbled by the fact that I was merely one of these many. The service ended with a robust singing of Cole Porter's song "Don't Fence Me In." It was a particular favorite of Emily's, who had been born and raised in the the wide open spaces of Oregon. She was a Westerner and remained one even as she constructed a happy life on the East Coast. The fact that this light-hearted anthem to Western values was written by Cole Porter made it a perfect blending of West and East.

In closing this account of my encounters with Bill and with his work, I would like to return to chapter 58 of *The Folded Leaf*; for me, again, the most beautiful and mysterious passage in Bill's most compelling novel. After having mentioned that much in the real world outside of us cannot be apprehended at all without the help of both the senses of sight and hearing, and that most of us are metaphorically deaf and blind, Bill chides, as previously mentioned, the eminently good-hearted Mrs. Forbes as an exemplar of this deafness and blindness. She sees in Mr Peters only a man who is becoming prematurely fat as he ages.

Next, in an exquisite and surprising shift, Maxwell suggests that only those who are actually blind or deaf can pick up on invisible inward feelings, such as the pain that Mr Peters is experiencing.

> A person really blind might have heard it in his step, a deaf person could have seen it in the way he turned his face to the sun.

For the blind and the deaf, of course, their remaining sense, either of sound or of sight, becomes almost preternaturally powerful. It seems to me that Bill is suggesting here not only that those who themselves live in the desert can sense the inner lives of others who live in it, but also that the particularity intense, intuitive, remaining sense can pick up on frequencies that are not available to others. This suggests that the particular wounds of an artist are also the source of his or her peculiar artistic strengths—a notion addressed many years ago by Edmund Wilson in his book *The Wound and the Bow*. More broadly, the preternatural insight referred to in this passage provides a metaphor for the kind of felt intuition that is required of great poets and of their readers.

Finally, I would like to revisit Bill's reference in the opening of the chapter 58 to a life that simply continues, without beginning or ending, without a past or a future, which indifferently works through human beings just as it works through rivers and even stones—although we are ordinarily at best only subliminally aware of it. For those with ears to hear, however, it can be heard in the quotidian unselfconscious activities of man, which give it a kind of inarticulate voice.

And yet at the same time, something deeper and more mysterious is happening. When I first read this passage, my eyes welled up with tears; for me, a very rare occurrence. I felt overwhelmed by a feeling that was not, as one might have expected, sadness, say sadness at man's being adrift in a world whose ongoing life is indifferent to his sufferings. Instead, or additionally, Bill's words put me in touch with something else, something seemingly undefinable.

My aforementioned guru's teachings were based on a tantric tradition now called by scholars the non-dual Shaivism of Kashmir, whose most prominent, systematic exponent was the medieval Kashmiri sage and metaphysician Abhinavagupta, who also remains, to this day, India's foremost theorist of aesthetics. In responding to works of art, we are also, according to Abhinavagupta, responding to a deep vein of feeling, which he calls *shanta rasa*. This profound vein of ineffable feeling is like a subtle but powerful current that underlies not only all of our particular, quotidian emotions in the so-called real world but also all of the other *rasas*, all of the other evocations of subtle, aesthetic feeling that arise and subside in our experience of works of art. Its essential nature, if it is to be named at all, is akin to the peace, in Christian terms, that passeth understanding, or to the Aristotelian notion of the catharsis of emotion that is effectuated by Greek tragedy. It is likened by Abhinavagupta to the unbroken continuum of Consciousness itself. The continuous force that Bill both describes and enacts at the beginning of chapter 58 signifies, it seems to me, not only nature's indifference to man but something deeper, more ineffable, something beyond signification, which is intuitively felt, not intellectually grasped, and whose very indifference can be experienced as a kind of joyful gift.

The term *same-hearted*, which is embedded in the title of the first section of this book, is the literal English equivalent of a Sanskrit term that is central to Abhinavagupta's aesthetic theory. It emphasizes the reader's or spectator's intuitive apprehension of works of art in response to the creative intuition that has produced them. To be a same-hearted reader of a great poem, or of any worthy work of art, requires not only intellectual insight but also felt intuition akin to that experienced by its maker. It is through a number of such felt intuitions that a reader's or spectator's capacity to apprehend works of art grows. Finally, felt intuition, however it is developed, provides insight into the actual state of affairs in the real world and is useful both in orienting us toward that world and in generating appropriate responses to the shifting landscapes with which it confronts us. Great art is the product of felt intuition that sinks its roots deep into the stuff of our lives and then re-emerges from them, in the process subtly transforming us.

As I reread chapter 58 of *The Folded Leaf*, I recall that in my meetings with Bill, we were each other's same-hearted readers and same-hearted listeners, aligned with some force, some continuum, that included but transcended us both.

At some point after his and Emily's funeral, I wrote an elegy for Bill. Its import should, given what I have written here, be relatively straightforward. One missing piece of information, alas, is relevant. The death of Bill's mother, like Bill's funeral, occurred in midsummer. Or perhaps, resorting to poetic license, I have revised history and have, for the purposes of the poem, simply presumed that her death occurred in midsummer.

DOUBLE ELEGY

In Memory of William Maxwell
Whose Mother Died When He Was Ten

One summer day the day was vaporized.
The color bled from the sky and all went white.
You lay down in that dazzle and tried to cry.

An invisible wave broke over you. You stayed.
It kept on going and has never stopped.
"No life is free of sorrow," the pastor said.

God never lived and so has never died.
Yet feeling, discrete, continuous, abides,
Keeps threatening or promising to break through.

You can't contain it. It envelopes you
As fragile as you are, as unbreakable.
Like one going blind who knows for the first time

The pathos of the visible, yet neither exults nor despairs,
You learned, with time, to shape this shifting scene.
In which, although departed, you remain

And leave us with no need nor wish to pray.
You bequeath us a no less dazzling summer day.

Just as I was completing the above section on Bill, a section from a longish poem called "Via Dolorosa," which I completed several years ago, flashed before my mind. The poem has a peculiar premise. A commuter who is heading home, from East to West, decides, out of a kind of despair, not to return home but simply to keep on going, headed West. Eventually, of course, he/she arrives at a desert, in which much of the poem is set. It occurred to me that this portion of the poem is similar to desert places of the spirit evoked by chapter 58 of *The Folded Leaf*. Often one is not aware, when writing a poem, of all of its occult influences. The stanzas on the desert seemed to simply rise, full-blown, into my mind. Now it seems to me that I must have had Bill's passage on the desert at the back of my mind while writing it. I include, below, a sample of the relevant portions of the poem. Portions elided are indicated by an elongated dash.

FROM VIA DOLOROSA

The road changes/ The road does not change.
Always, at noon, the sun shimmers.
Time seems to stand still. It seems too early
To be the middle of the day. I imagine

I am holding fine grains of sand in my hand.
Sifting through them, I am surprised
How different each appears, as though
Deposited here in different epochs

Forming different strata. Time, in a scale
Too vast to comprehend, is buried here.
The sun, already past its apogee, descends
Toward the perfect line of the horizon...

———————-

Out here the air is so thick you can almost see
Its wavering eddies. Tumbleweeds,
Like the ghost of some unknown substance,
Dance on the limitless sands of no shore.

I wonder, what must it be like to surrender
To the vagaries of the wind, to a force,
Invisible, whose motions are entirely random.
Each instant unique and unrepeatable

The road does not change/ The road changes.
Still I exist at the border between worlds—
The emptiness within, the emptiness without
Abide with their own secret life.

I am not blind. The desert can become sublime,
Overwhelming the mind as surely as any
Mountain, like the Alps a tourist once traversed,
Unawares, first elated, then let down.

Minimalism stakes its claim: bleached bones
Bare against sand; darting birds, tiny,
Particolored; the sentinel sun, and silence,
And the whirring hum of insects.

The road changes/ The road does not change.
Out here the seasons no longer revolve.
Out here the weather scarcely changes.
Random clouds drift by overhead.

Now and then a gas station, brightly colored.
A single pump. A single boy attending it.
Like a painting by Edward Hopper. Materialized
From nowhere. Stations along the way.

From where has he come? Perhaps from a town
Obscured by a hill. But here there are no hills.
How very proud his parents must be of him!
Still just a boy, yet earning his keep.

The road does not change/ The road changes.
A mirage before us, a mirage behind us,
And silence, silence humming like an engine,
Droning its high-pitched AUM

3. Robert Fitzgerald

I will now turn my attention to Robert Fitzgerald, yet another mentor who was a same-hearted reader of both me and ultimately, as I only later found out, of my work. Although I did not know it at the time, it turned out, in what seemed another extraordinary coincidence, that Fitzgerald and Maxwell had been roommates who lived together in an apartment off-campus when Fitzgerald was an undergraduate and Maxwell a graduate student at Harvard. They became close friends. At the time Fitzgerald, though the younger of the two, had the natural authority of an elder. When they met, Maxwell was an aspiring poet. It was Fitzgerald who, with the frankness of a true friend, risked suggesting to Maxwell that he should concentrate on prose, not poetry.

I have discovered, too, that there were striking similarities between Fitzgerald's and Maxwell's early lives. Both were born and raised in small towns in southern Illinois. Fitzgerald's mother, too, died when he was young, when in fact he was only three years old. An older brother, his only sibling, died at the age of five, significantly compounding his sense of loss. And so he, like Bill, grew up under the care and supervision of his father. In the case of Fitzgerald, his father suffered throughout his adult life, like Euripides' tragic hero Philoctetes in his play of the same name, from a suppurating wound in his hip that refused to heal. This pain preoccupied Fitzgerald's father and enforced a certain distance between him and his son. While a senior at Harvard, Fitzgerald played the lead role in *Philoctetes*, a role which must have involved considerable bravery to assume.

Later in life, Fitzgerald wrote a brief account of his childhood. In some ways his prose, both tonally and with respect to the world it conjures forth, is similar to Maxwell's, but it is also in significant ways quite different. Fitzgerald's father became an alcoholic, and while drunk, he became quite terrifying to his children, a figure entirely different from the kind, forbearing, though often preoccupied father that he was when sober. There is an anguished ambivalence in Fitzgerald's account of his childhood that is absent from Bill's mostly idealized portraits of his own. After recounting the terror and confusion with which he responded to his father's behavior, Fitzgerald writes:

> There should be a reticent surface to life, but I must allow phantasma like these to break it if I am to make myself in any serious way intelligible. No general view of things would ever seem just to me unless it comprehended Heaven and Hell—a range in experience at least as great as that between my exaltations as a child and my glimpses of anguish and evil.

Here Fitzgerald's range seems greater than Bill's, whose childhood, as portrayed in his fiction, seems always to be bathed, retrospectively, in the glow of a kind of innocence. Bill never addresses in his writing the question of evil, just as, again unlike Fitzgerald, he never betrays any interest in matters spiritual, which he simply dismisses out of hand, or which, rather, likely never assumed for him a sufficient significance to occasion a formal dismissal.

Fitzgerald wrote movingly of his final and profound reconciliation with his father.

> He did not die when they thought he would, and after that there was a kind of adjustment or quiescence of illness when he even seemed to mend, so that invalid though he was, he no longer had constant pain. My mother and my brother had been taken from me; now my father was given to me, and the gift was beyond estimation. He was freed now of his bitter demon, restored to himself and to patience, unconscious of his own courage, utterly without spiritual side. He had everything to impart, as I had everything to learn, of the discipline, humility, and humor proper to a man.

Among the things that Fitzgerald's father did not impart to him, that Fitzgerald must have somehow discovered on his own, was a "spiritual side." Like Ponsot, he was a devout Catholic, and like her this was an aspect of his experience which he in no way advertised. Only as a result of reading his brief memoir did I learn that for Fitzgerald, a life of prayer was inextricably a part of life in general.

Though Fitzgerald, while at Harvard, occupied an endowed chair with a long history and an august title, "The Boylston Professor of Rhetoric and Oratory," his prestige among student writers lagged behind that of Bishop, and especially that of Robert Lowell, who was considered top dog at the time. Fitzgerald was certainly respected and was also widely regarded as kind and courteous. He taught what was at least a somewhat legendary course on prosody, one which I was foolish enough not to take, opting instead for his creative writing seminar.

Fitzgerald's presence had exactly the qualities that one might expect, or rather hope, would grace one who was both a poet and a scholar of classics. He had a noble, slightly craggy but handsome face, which when seen in profile looked somehow Roman. One could imagine it on the side of an ancient coin. His manner, though reserved, was not aloof. He was a master of understatement and sometimes, if one looked hard, his eyes had a kind of ironic twinkle. It was not a manner that either encouraged or discouraged intimacy. Unlike Bishop, he seemed to enjoy teaching. He seemed, too, thoroughly unfazed by the unwashed and long-haired hordes, the mostly gentle, young Visigoths, anything but classical, who invaded his classroom.

Fitzgerald kept liberal office hours and encouraged us to make use of them. During my first meeting with him, he examined one of the spiky, sharp-elbowed, free-verse poems that I was producing at the time. I remember his eyes lifting from the page, peering over his reading glasses, as he announced his summary judgement: "*I PREFER THE RIPE PEACH*." This pronouncement, which out of context seems affected and pompous, was delivered with a hint of dry, mock orotundity and with the aforementioned ironic twinkle in his eye.

I continued to take advantage of Fitzgerald's office hours, during which he began to exhibit slightly, just slightly, more solicitude toward my work. At the same time, something far more important was transpiring. I began to feel that Fitzgerald was not only fond of me but genuinely interested in me as a person—an experience heretofore unprecedented in my collegiate academic career. The rest of the Harvard grandees whose path I had crossed had scarcely noticed me. This interest was not communicated in any obvious way. I experienced it, initially, through the kind of felt intuition to which I have earlier referred, and only slightly later through the somewhat more evident care, attention, and respect with which he listened and then responded to whatever I said. I, in turn, began to listen to him with a similar care, although our taste in poetry, by which I confess I mostly mean *my* poetry, did not always coincide. We, too, had become, in effect, same-hearted readers of each other. Fitzgerald's office hours became a cherished respite for me. I was sad, of course, when the class ended.

Fitzgerald was not only a renowned translator but also a poet. He published three well-received books of poetry written over four decades and later collected them, along with additional poems, in his volume *Spring Shade*. No less exacting a critic than Harold Bloom, in his voluminous and rather grandiose work *The Western Canon*, chose one of Fitzgerald's books of poetry, *A Wreath For The Sea*, in his supplemental list of twentieth-century works that might someday attain canonical status.

Fitzgerald's poems reveal his mastery of prosody. They are eloquent and grave, unremittingly yet unpretentiously serious. They gesture frequently and often painfully toward his Christian faith as well as to persons and places that haunt the world of Greek myth and literature. Unsurprisingly, in the case of one whose first book was published in 1930 and who was a devout Catholic, Fitzgerald's poems, at times, echo those of the Anglican Eliot. The two men shared a necessarily distant transatlantic bond of mutual friendship and respect.

Somewhat more surprisingly, Fitzgerald was a close friend of John Berryman— the same Berryman whose frequent drunken indiscretions famously scandalized Miss Bishop. Berryman was not only a poet and critic but also a scholar whose painstaking emended edition of *King Lear*, a labor of love that was always an unfinished work in progress, and of Stephen Crane's *The Red Badge of Courage*, are still respected by other scholars to this day. Berryman, in short, was deeply serious about his work as a poet and was also, according to the testimony of many of his students, a passionate teacher of poetry who impressed upon them his view of poetry as an almost sacred calling, deserving of or rather demanding incessant hard labor and an attitude of reverent devotion.

It is upon this ground that one can imagine Fitzgerald and Berryman meeting, though I suspect Fitzgerald appreciated Berryman's sometimes scabrous humor as well. Most of Berryman's long poem, "Homage to Mistress Bradstreet"—which followed two decades of exacting but never quite realized formal poems, and which was a breakthrough in which he achieved, finally, his distinctive voice—was written while he was staying with Fitzgerald and his wife. With typical generosity, Fitzgerald wrote of "Mistress Bradstreet" and its author, "He has bided his time and written the poem of his generation."

It would be a regrettable omission not to include Fitzgerald's voice as a poet here. I will simply cite, first, a passage from Fitzgerald's poem "History," which his appropriately-named wife, Penelope, chose as an epigraph preceding her introduction to a posthumous collection of Fitzgerald's memoirs and works of criticism, and which she doubtless viewed as exemplary of Fitzgerald's poetry at its best; and then a relatively brief poem that I have chosen perhaps because its locale has nostalgic connotations for me, connotations of which Fitzgerald himself is a part.

FROM HISTORY

             ...   A man, this man
Bred among lakes and railway cars and smoke,
The salt of childhood on his wintry lips,
His full heart ebbing toward the new tide
Arriving, arriving, in laughter and cries,
Down the chaotic dawn and eastern drift,
Would hail the unforeseen, and celebrate
On the great mountainside those sprites,
Tongues of delight, that may remember him—
The yet unborn, trembling in the same rooms,
Breakfasting before the same gray windows,
Lying, grieving again; yet all beyond him,
Who knew he lived in rough Jehovah's breath,
And burned, a quiet wick in the wild night,
Loving what he beheld and will behold.

CHARLES RIVER NOCTURNE

Reflecting remote swords, chilled in the calm
And liquid darkness, lights on the esplanade
Prolong the night's edge downward all night long

To those whose nostrils ache with the strong darkness,

Those who in hunger press against the waters

Those without birth or death, to whom the cold
Ocean long laboring in her regal tomb
Whispers a word of foam.

                  The lavish cars
Move westward in an eddy and dance of shadow
Under the dazed lamps on the lifeless shore.

Both poems reflect the eloquent gravity to which I have referred earlier. Both, too, retain an aura of mystery. Who is the man to whom the first of the above poems refers? In the course of the poem, he becomes a mythic figure, a celebrant of mountaintop mysteries who is intimate with the still unborn, yet beyond all "lived in rough Jehovah's breath," in the life of the spirit, from which perspective he is enabled, though no more than "a quiet wick in the wild night," to view all things in both the present and future with love.

In "Charles River Nocturne," similarly, one wonders about the ontological status of those without birth or death, like those yet unborn in "History," to whom the ocean whispers, as it did to Whitman, its word of foam. Who are those who whose "nostrils ache with the strong darkness /... who in hunger press against the waters"? Regardless, they hint at some realm of the spirit beyond or other than the merely human. Further questions arise. Why are the lamps that line the shore personified, in an Eliot-like touch, as "dazed," and why is the shore itself "lifeless" under those lamps? Does the Charles River become a kind of earthly analogue to the Acheron?

Both poems reflect Fitzgerald's mastery of prosody. The first is one long, exquisitely modulated sentence with a supple and varied pentameter line. The second ends with a lovely, long glissando. Both poems are harbingers of Fitzgerald's use of a similarly varied and supple pentameter line in his translations of Homer's epics.

In my view, Fitzgerald's poems, though distinguished and humanly attractive, though characterized by a quiet, elegiac gravity that was reflective of their author, missing only his sly, ironic glints of humor, never quite cut loose and soar. They never achieve, despite or perhaps because of their fine decorum, a breakthrough into the assumption of a startlingly original and arresting voice. This estimation, like all such assessments, is provisional; perhaps Fitzgerald's poetry will find a receptive reader who will reintroduce his work at greater length than does Bloom.

While still actively engaged in writing poetry, Fitzgerald translated, along with a collaborator, Dudley Fitts, Sophocles' *Oedipus Rex*—which still seems to me to have an uncanny radiance and power unmatched by any subsequent translation—and later *Oedipus at Colonus* and *Antigone*. Given his relatively sparse output as a poet, an output that became still sparser in his later years, it seems that Fitzgerald realized that though an estimable poet, he was not likely to be a major one. If so, it was doubtless a painful realization. A true poet never ceases to be fundamentally a poet.

No longer concentrating primarily on his own work as a poet allowed Fitzgerald to train his full energies on what was a daunting undertaking, his translations of *The Odyssey*, *The Iliad*, and finally *The Aeneid*. I know no Greek or Latin, so I cannot vouch for the accuracy of Fitzgerald's translations, and I am, of course, predisposed to be prejudiced in his favor.

There are three translations of *The Odyssey* that are still routinely read, those by Fitzgerald and Richmond Lattimore, near contemporaries, and a subsequent translation by Robert Fagles. Lattimore's translation earns, for most critics, particularly high marks for its accuracy and faithfulness to the original, qualities that are also lauded in Fagles' version. Fitzgerald is seen by some as having taken perhaps a few too many liberties with the text.

One of those liberties is that Fitzgerald's translation has as its base the English pentameter line, which, as in his own poems, is elegantly and flexibly deployed. *The Iliad* and *The Odyssey*, in the original Greek, are composed in dactylic hexameter, whose lines vary from thirteen to seventeen syllables. It is a commonplace understanding, and a justifiable one, that lines of such length simply do not work in English; they become the equivalent of a series of logjams. It is difficult to sustain any momentum from one line to the next. Surely producing versions, particularly of poems, that work in the language into which they are translated is among the obligations of a translator. It seems to me that Lattimore's and Fagles' attempts to transpose Homer's long lines into English result in a kind of turgidity that should have been predictable and ought to have been avoided.

Fitzgerald's loose pentameter line simply works better in English; his translation, less dense and agglutinated than those of his competitors, also admits more space to circulate freely around and between his lines, qualities which seem to me eminently Greek. The omnipresence of space, too, is experienced by those who travel by sea. In sum, Fitzgerald's *Odyssey* is a far better poem in English and is perhaps in spirit closer to Homer than are those of his competitors, which, as Fitzgerald was himself both a poet and a lifelong student of prosody, is unsurprising. Fitzgerald's version, though now read less widely, still remains in print more than a half a century after its first appearance.

My last memory of Fitzgerald is a particularly vivid one. He had just finished his version of *The Iliad*. He was ready, for the first time, to read excerpts from it, and the date and place had been arranged. Hence I and about five hundred others were crowded into the largest lecture hall in Harvard—with the exception of the cavernous Sanders Theater, which had famously poor acoustics. The mood in the room can only be described as one of rapt, slightly tense, anticipation.

Fitzgerald entered a few minutes late. He was wearing the crumpled houndstooth hat that he often sported. Sensing the mood in the room, he headed not for the podium but instead, mysteriously, to a side wall. He removed his hat from his head and then attempted several times to hang it on a non-existent peg, finally giving up with a kind of mock frustration. In response to this little Chaplinesque pantomime, yet another instance of Fitzgerald's understated humor, a wave of laughter swept over the room, as a result of which all the tension in the room dissipated. In retrospect, it seemed to me that something of the essence of Fitzgerald was condensed and expressed in this brief, cathartic feint. I do not think for a moment that he cooked up his little pantomime before he entered the lecture hall. Rather, I think he simply read the atmosphere in the room and then responded in the moment with a perfectly appropriate gesture.

As it happens this account, too, has a happy, coincidental postscript. Several years after I graduated from Harvard, a friend of mine showed me a book of which I had previously been completely unaware, despite the fact that it had been in print for almost two years. The book was called *First Flowering*. It was an anthology of the fledgling work of various novelists and poets of note, including my beloved Stevens, as well as Eliot, Cummings, Conrad Aiken, and many others, that had first appeared in *The Harvard Advocate*. I had been a member of the *Advocate* while at Harvard, and its threadbare, never renovated, poorly heated, and terminally scruffy confines had become a kind of refuge for me.

During my last year at Harvard, I had finished writing a long poem, "The Fall of Miss Alaska," thirteen pages in typescript, in a manner only slightly less spiky than the poems I had shown Fitzgerald. Among the student editors and others who had read it, it was considered, to my delight, a kind of unreservedly triumphant *tour de force*. My stock as a poet had precipitously risen among my peers. The poem was accepted for publication but would appear in a Fall issue of *The Harvard Advocate* that was to come out after my graduation. At that point my life had moved on, and knowing that I was definitively outside of the charmed circle of young poets who had been my peers, I knew also that I would be unlikely to hear from them.

The friend who had brought *First Flowering* to my belated attention excitedly told me to look at its final pages. The long poem to which I have referred was there reproduced in its entirety. It was the last piece in the book. No other work from *The*

Harvard Advocate's previous ten or so years had been included. Again, the primary mandate of the magazine was to include the work of figures later recognized as luminaries. I was anything but.

But my happiest surprise came when I glanced at the cover of the book and discovered that Norman Mailer and Robert Fitzgerald—an unlikely duo—had been its editors, charged with curating and selecting its entries.

It was clear to me that Fitzgerald had both selected my long, still somewhat eccentrically shaped poem and had given it pride of place as the last poem in the volume. Fitzgerald would not have included the poem had he not been impressed by it, so it pleased me that I had finally produced something that had passed muster. More importantly, I was touched and moved by this final, silent gesture of approval from a figure whom I had come to love and revere.

I never asked Maxwell about whether or to what extent his relationship with Fitzgerald had been ongoing. Maxwell outlived Fitzgerald by two and a half decades. Fitzgerald died at the relatively young age of seventy-four, scarcely a decade after I had come to know him.

Beginning in my early thirties, wishing to explore new poetic possibilities, I began the rather long and arduous task of teaching myself how to write in form. Though no master of prosody, I now feel relatively comfortable writing both in free verse and in form. I would like to think of this as well as the words you have just read as a belated tribute on my part to Fitzgerald.

~ CHAPTER 2 ~

ERICK HAWKINS: THE DANCER AND THE DANCE

1.

It seems to me that individuals, virtually all individuals, wish in some way to be acknowledged, which, broken down to its component parts, means that they wish to be seen rather than to be looked at, and to be listened to rather than merely heard. It seems to me that the world would be a more graceful place were one, as an individual, to attempt to remind oneself to really see people rather than simply to look at them, were one to attempt to remind oneself simply to listen to people rather than merely to hear them, were one to treat, in other words, others as sovereign individuals, as persons, rather than as personified objects to be either ignored or manipulated.

I am by no means claiming that I am a paragon who has performed this particular form of spiritual practice with any regularity in my life. Alas, I have not. However, I have listened to individuals as sovereign individuals enough to know that when one does so, they are never—no, *never*—boring. Every individual is a miraculous center of consciousness who bestows surprising gifts, nuances of thought and feeling, or unforeseen qualities of character that, when assimilated, become part of one's own available stock of reality. If one makes the effort to consciously attend to others as sovereign individuals, they will flower, revealing themselves as startlingly interesting, and one will flower oneself.

My favorite of Blake's aphorisms in the *Marriage of Heaven and Hell* is quite direct and un-metaphorical: "The most sublime act is to set another before you." What Blake beautifully refers to as "set[ting] another before oneself" involves a voluntary act of conscious awareness, a subtle shift in one's habitual orientation toward another through which one apprehends him or her not, as it were, reflected darkly in the mirror of one's refractory unconsciousness, but face to face, as one sovereign individual to another. For Blake the human form, when seen consciously, becomes "the human form divine," the most beautiful and sublime of all forms.

I have spent far more of my life living unconsciously than consciously, far more in forgetting than remembering. It is perhaps too much to expect of oneself that one will constantly remind oneself to truly acknowledge, to see and listen to others. Often one needs to be reminded to wake up from the slumber of unconsciousness either by preceptors, spiritual or secular, or by others who insist upon being seen and acknowledged as sovereign individuals, who insist, in effect, that one wake up. Sometimes these will be gurus, sometimes political figures, sometimes family members or friends. And sometimes they will be artists.

According to Abhinavagupta, one can have this experience of waking up through art, through poetry, or through dramatic works that are works not only of skill but of genius, that inspire in spectators stirrings of same-hearted, intuitive identification not only with the spirit of whoever has authored such works, but in the case of drama, which for him as for Aristotle is the paradigmatic art form, also the actors, often extraordinarily skilled, sometimes themselves geniuses, who perform them.

My first experience of being deeply moved by a work of art occurred when I was ten or eleven years old. I watched a televised version of *Death of a Salesman* featuring truly inspired—for me definitive and unforgettable—performances by Lee J. Cobb and Mildred Dunnock. As I watched, I felt myself being overcome by a kind of feeling I had never before experienced. I felt, on the one hand, devastated and overwhelmed, heartbroken by what I was seeing and hearing, but on the other hand quietly elated by it. One line in the play stood out for me above all others. It seemed to my still childish mind to articulate the essence of what the play was conveying. Willy Loman's wife says, referring to her husband: "Attention must be paid." I won't belabor the fact that this line is about truly acknowledging another, about being fully aware, about being conscious, and about being one with Consciousness as love, as the intelligence of the heart. It is also, of course, about listening.

When the play was over, I felt exhausted, but the feeling that it evoked in me remained. Indeed, it has never left me. Perhaps in a way it articulated my own desperate need at the time to be acknowledged. So many children, lacking parents who are able to provide such acknowledgement, feel the need of it. It seems to me that the capacity of children to be deeply moved by mature works of art is vastly underappreciated.

Years later, I saw what is now a legendary production of O'Neill's *A Moon for the Misbegotten,* starring Jason Robards and Colleen Dewhurst, which I found overwhelming in much the same way I had found *Death of a Salesman* overwhelming as a child. Robards and Dewhurst entirely inhabited their harrowing roles. Again, the performances of actors and dancers can themselves be acts of genius, and the performances of Robards and Dewhurst, and of Cobb and Dunnok, were such acts.

Over and over again, even in mediocre plays, I have seen actors thoroughly invest themselves in their roles. I have had, literally only once, the experience of an actor "mailing it in" in a performance. I find the dedication of actors, their determination under all circumstances to give it their all, both gallant and touching. There is something, too, about actors being physically before us in plays that adds a dimension not found in movies. Somehow, the bodily presence of actors whom we are engaged in scrutinizing, hopefully in truly seeing, entails a kind of vulnerability that we all implicitly share.

Finally, performances of plays are, of course, ephemeral. They vanish as soon as they are over. Even legendary productions of plays live on only in the memories of those who have seen them, until they too vanish. There is something about actors' wholehearted commitment to that which is not destined to last that is also a commitment to abiding, at least for awhile, in the present. Similarly, perhaps, all of our lives are in some sense performances that are not destined to last, and our investment of ourselves in them, even as we realize their transience—in some sense even perhaps *because* we recognize that transience—likewise involves a kind of gallantry.

Watching dramatic performances, unlike reading poems or novels, involves not only same-hearted listening but same-hearted seeing. That seeing is largely focussed upon actors who have the capacity to draw the audience into the play. They help us, in the words of the blinded Gloucester in *King Lear*, to "see feelingly," to become same-hearted seers. Attending to live performances of plays thus involves both same-hearted listening and same-hearted seeing

Watching plays or dance performances not only exposes us to the genius—or lack of it—of the playwright or choreographer but also to that of the actors or dancers who are charged with realizing their visions. The kind of vulnerability of the actor's physical presence before an audience is greatly magnified in the case of dancers, who usually have no lines to speak and who for the most part, in modern dance, have no roles behind which to hide. They are simply bodily present before an audience in a position of radical vulnerability that involves not only gallantry but also a kind of bravery.

2.

Both gallantry and bravery were exhibited by the last of my series of exemplary mentors, the one with whom I felt perhaps the strongest bond, the great dancer and choreographer Erick Hawkins. I was privileged to encounter Erick because my father had met and become close friends with him during a summer session at Bennington College when both were in their mid-thirties. Erick was in the early stages of his career as a choreographer. Pictures taken of his dance performances during that time reveal an almost preternaturally beautiful young man. A number of years later, my father became the chairman of the board of Erick's dance company and remained so for almost thirty years. My father had no real interest in dance but accepted his role out of affection and loyalty to Erick.

About dance I know, properly speaking, too little, but enough to know that, apart from or alongside poetry, dance and architecture are the art forms to which I feel most attracted, with which I feel most attuned.

This has caused me, quite naturally, to ponder what the nexus might be between dance, architecture, and poetry. We are all of us, as humans, embodied beings, and our bodies are both vehicles and expressions of the spirit. Just as the spirit, in a sense, dwells in our bodies, so our bodies dwell in buildings, whose lineaments are likewise realized in a concrete, material form.

In Renaissance architecture, buildings were patterned after the proportions of the body. Poetry was originally and to some degree still is a spoken, bodily art form in which a myriad of physical processes are involved in the production and projection of the voice. Moreover, poetry's rhythms are intimately connected with the incoming and outgoing breath, with the systole and diastole of the heartbeat, and also with a subtle internal or overt external motion. Essential to poetry, more than is usually recognized, is a kinesthetic dimension. The simplest expression of this is the fact that walking, likewise a rhythmic exercise, has been recognized by many poets as an aid to poetic inspiration.

Poems, as written down, have their own form of materiality. Unlike more abstract forms of discourse, they, too, deal with the stubbornly concrete, with what Blake, who proclaimed that "to generalize is to be an idiot," called "minute particulars." Indeed all art forms, but perhaps preeminently dance, are in some way intimately connected with the body, with Blake's "human form divine."

Erick grew up in rural Colorado near a Native American reservation. He became familiar with tribal rituals in which dance played a vital role and to some extent assimilated the ethos, the spiritual purport expressed by these dances. Erick wrote that as he began his life as a dancer,

> ...I knew that I would never be happy until I had found a way to make dance for all Americans part of a concept of totality... I knew that I could never again make a distinction between the sacred and the profane.

A brilliant student, Erick was granted a full scholarship to Harvard, where he majored in classics. Classical themes, motifs, and myths are frequently evoked in Erick's dances. In striving to articulate, through dance, his vision of totality, Erick developed a deep interest in Eastern spirituality and aesthetics. A notoriously difficult book, F. S. C. Northrop's *The Meeting of East and West*, which in part compares Western and Eastern aesthetics, became for Erick a kind of bible, one which he suggested that I and others read, but which was too dense and intricate for me to grasp.

Erick engaged in a lively epistolary conversation with Northrop. Two other major influences on his thinking were D. T. Suzuki, an early and brilliant exponent of Zen Buddhism, and the Catholic philosopher Jaques Maritain. The eclecticism of these influences suggest something of the intensity of Erick's intellectual and spiritual search for an articulation of his vision of totality.

Finally, Erick developed an equally deep and crucial interest in kinesiology, in the emerging science of the study of the movement of the human body. These four strings or strands—the Native American, the classical, the kinesiological, and the study of Eastern spirituality—along with his far-ranging reading and his own unique and unknowable experience of life, were woven together seamlessly in Erick's work as a choreographer.

For Erick dance itself was a spiritual practice. He wrote:

> ... how we dance springs from our total philosophic view of our human life, and, insofar as our philosophic idea is partial or has gaps in it, our dance can be stiffened and set, become limited or only partially functioning. ...If the dance is to be of excellence and vitality, and if it is to be a metaphor of our existence, then we have to consider what good existence is, or even what existence is, period. ...So my conclusion is if you want to arrive at quality—real intensity and real excitement in the art of dance—you have to look at real quality in existence.

Once again a vision of totality is paramount here, as is an imaginative/intellectual/spiritual resistance to the fixed, the set, and the categorical, and an openness to the dynamic, to the fluid, to the freely flowing. But there is, in addition, a concern with ontology, with *being* itself, from which arises the question of what *good* being is, an attempt to look at real quality in existence.

F. S. C. Northrop was one of the first thinkers to engage in an exploration of what are now called *qualia*, which pertain to the felt nature of our subjective, sensory intuitions of phenomena like the color blue or of physical pain. Why we experience such subjective states as we do is now called by philosophers of science and others the hard problem of consciousness, because no current materialistic theory of consciousness can account for them.

Erick's concern with quality, mediated through Northrop, was remarkably prescient. But Erick also thought of quality in a more general sense, involving the old, largely Greek philosophical question of what a good life is and how to lead such a life. Ultimately, of course, Erick was engaged throughout his whole life in exploring how "real quality in existence" might best be expressed, incarnated, in dance, in the movement of the human body itself.

Erick's life, in his single-minded, unwavering pursuit of necessarily provisional answers to these questions—answers expressed in dance—was stripped of all that was inessential. He lived a life of almost monastic poverty.

Hawkins was a self-consciously, fiercely, defiantly American artist. The generation immediately preceding that of Hawkins was the heyday of what is now called Modernism. Among American poets, there was a rift between those, like Eliot and Pound, who left America in their early twenties and assimilated themselves to European culture and its traditions, and those who, like Wallace Stevens and William Carlos Williams, remained stubbornly on native ground. Clearly, Hawkins cast his lot with the latter.

Hawkins, however, came of age as an artist at a time when the avant-garde, represented by such figures as John Cage and Merce Cunningham, was itself beginning to become ascendant. But the avant-garde, too, was originally a European phenomenon, later grafted, with varying degrees of success, in part by those fleeing Europe, onto the American cultural scene.

Eventually, however, as is often the case, the avant-garde migrated from its marginal position and became, for many, eccentrically central, and then itself became mainstream. This was particularly true of the visual arts in which abstract expressionists—who, like Erick, strove to seek an essentially American art—were supplanted by Warhol and his successors, whose cynically manipulative version of the avant-garde and all that followed it quickly routed the cultural field, transforming the visual arts into a rapidly appreciating commodity hoarded by wealthy collectors, as a result of which other forms of expression came to seem marginal, outmoded, and quaintly conventional.

Though Hawkins' work was contemporaneous with the emergence of an Americanized avant-garde, his aesthetic, as we have seen, was fed by many other streams as well. His work was never embraced by critics whose sensibility, like the artists whom they critiqued and promoted, was more narrowly avant-garde. Erick's work, unlike that of Cunningham, was for the most part overlooked by such critics. His repertoire or semiotics of movements natural to the body seemed to them too repetitive, too simple and un-flamboyant, too organic. His later work, however, was finally and unreservedly granted its due by critics who took their cue from Anna Kisselgoff, who became the lead dance critic of *The New York Times* in 1977, and who had a deep understanding of and appreciation for Erick's work.

3.

What might it have meant for Hawkins to be a self-consciously American choreographer? I will approach this question as I have begun to broach it above by way of analogy to what I know, which is to say, by way of looking at several poets, and one novelist, specifically at Whitman, Melville, William Carlos Williams, and

Charles Olson, all of whom, unlike Pound and Eliot, were self-consciously American authors in ways that are analogous to Hawkins' attitude and practice.

America was and is, of course, still a relatively young country with a limited temporal horizon, but for much of her history, she has had an almost limitless *spatial* horizon, with vast tracts of still undiscovered, still unexplored terrain. The newness of America and its spaciousness required, it seemed—for example, to Whitman—a new aesthetic, one that stressed the spatial over the temporal, a predilection reflected not only in his long, geographically inclusive catalogues, in his many songs of the open road, and in his love of the vastness, the outsized scale of America itself, but also in the structure of his greatest poems. *Song of Myself* is a long poem, which, after it was completed, was subdivided by Whitman into numbered passages. Most critics of the poem make the mistake of interpreting these sections as though they represent some kind of coherent temporal unfolding, some orderly, progressive argument, though just how one is told to group its sequences and follow its argument varies widely from critic to critic. As I have argued in my essay on Whitman in another book, the organizing principle of *Song of Myself* is spatial not temporal. The poem moves from a kind of unbounded circumference to circles of increasingly limited scope that are nested within it and within each other, like a series of Chinese boxes, all parts of one vast continuum ranging from vast galaxies, through man, to a blade of grass, with no segment of the continuum—even the most vast—privileged over the others.

Similarly, the poet Charles Olson, in his ground-breaking study on Melville, *Call Me Ishmael*, argues that a wide-open sense of space, in Melville's case the sometimes literally maddening vastness of the ocean rather than that of a terrestrial wilderness, is the one essential fact.

Olson himself, like Williams and Hawkins, stressed, but more self-consciously, the spatial over the temporal. His notion of "composition by field," of using the entire space of the page in articulating poems, was similar to the "all over" technique of abstract expressionism, which availed itself of the entire canvas and which, in its lack of differentiation between the high and the low, between surface and and depth, and in its refusal to dictate a privileged direction, any implicit route or road map for the eye to follow, likewise privileged space over any orderly temporal unfolding. One takes in these paintings synoptically, as a totality of brush strokes, all at once, just as one takes in spaces, natural vistas, a-temporally, all at once. Again, the abstract expressionists, unlike the many avant-garde artists—from Jasper Johns to Warhol and beyond—who followed them, even or perhaps especially those who had fled or migrated from Europe, defined themselves, like Erick, Williams, and Olson, in contradistinction to European models, attempting to express something genuinely new and distinctively American.

Olson took the radical step of rejecting the whole history of European culture from the pre-Socratics onward as an unfortunate detour into ratiocination, abstract thinking, conceptual categorization, and in general to the laying down of definitions at the expense of a more open-ended, tentative yet probing, exploratory orientation toward the world, one responsive to new possibilities, fresh discoveries. For Olson, a cardinal sin of the abstract mind is its tendency to externally impose its fixed, airtight categories upon phenomena—in a process that Wordsworth, likewise sensitive to the sometimes destructive depredations of the rational mind, called "murdering to dissect"—rather than patiently waiting for phenomena, ever changing, ever arising and subsiding, to disclose their lineaments, always provisional, always themselves changing, as it were, from within.

Olson, who at 6 feet, 9 inches tall was a giant of a man, chose as his poetic sobriquet "Maximus." For Olson, who doubtless had to be alert to the low lying lintels of doors and other hindrances and hazards of an environment not built to his scale, the human body and its actual, concrete contact with the world was the prime instrument of genuine discovery. More than conceptualization, more even than perception, Olson stressed proprioception, the body's sense of its movement through space and its unmediated physical contact with reality, as the primary datum of human experience.

Olson went on numerous extended field trips to Mexico. He felt that he found in the remnants, the ruins, of Mayan culture—among which, despite his large frame, he literally crawled—and in particular in its hieroglyphs concretely graven in stone, evidence of a society in which direct contact with reality was prized and actualized. It was not, finally, of importance whether Olson's vision of Mayan society was anthropologically or culturally sound. As an enthusiast, not a scholar, it was enough for him that these ruins were a revelation, and that they resulted in poems such as "The Kingfishers," his most uncannily compelling work.

It is worth noting here that Melville, Olson's great hero, set out on his first whaling voyage as a very young man after the finances of his once securely upper-middle-class family had collapsed. This voyage was the essential formative experience of his life. At one point, he jumped ship in what was then the South Sea Islands and spent the better part of what was for him an idyllic year before being rescued by another whaler, living among its natives, who accepted him first as an honored guest, then quickly as one of their own, and whose culture, pacific in more ways than one, Melville came to regard as more civilized than of the contemporaneous West.

All of which brings us back to Hawkins. And to what it meant for him to be American. The sources or stimulants of his vision—classical, Eastern, Native American, and kinesiological—were, of course, different from those of Olson. Brought up in Colorado at a time when it was still a frontier, he remained at heart a Westerner, nurtured on vast open spaces, which he carried within him just as many artists carry their childhood into adulthood. There was nothing affected, nothing of the sometimes refined and etiolated Easterner about Erick. Like poets—from Whitman and Melville through Williams to Olson—before him, and like artists from the Hudson River school to Jackson Pollock, he maintained in his art the primacy of an open, uncluttered, clear sense of space, inviting endless discovery, that he associated with being American.

Dance is, among other things, the articulation of space by the human body. For Erick, it was essential that this space remain open and uncluttered, that it include even its correlative, emptiness. His focus on kinesiology, like Olson's focus on proprioception, mandated movements that were proper and natural to the body as an instrument of discovery, not movements forced upon it from without. There was for Erick and for Olson an essential connection between a clear sense of *space* and a vital, viable, clear sense of *place*—the place that was for Olson the *polis* undistorted by the ratiocination and the disfiguring force of a capitalism grounded in abstraction, a force opposed to the value of the concrete particularity of the world and direct—even fundamentally tactile—contact with it.

Erick, likewise, sought a space and a culture through which the body could move with the intrinsic dignity proper to it, and he decried any penchant toward coercion and control that would force the body to assume and often hold onto unnatural, fixed positions, the analogue of a Western culture wedded to the fixed and the categorical.

Erick's aesthetic, like that of Taoism, with which he was familiar, was not one of grimly holding on but of joyfully releasing and letting go. Much of Western culture seemed to him to be governed by precisely the kind of coercive force mandated from outside or above that he condemned, to be governed by an attitude prizing a kind of tortured virtuosity, which in the case of dance regarded the body as an obstacle to be overcome, to be broken into shape, and eventually, when thoroughly broken by age and debility, to be discarded.

For many years, Erick was not only the principal but the sole male dancer in Martha Graham's company. During much of that time, they were married. Graham's dances were often rooted in classical myth. The extent to which Erick, with his training in the classics, may have influenced her work is seldom if ever discussed. At some point, however, he felt the need to strike out on his own as a choreographer.

The bodies of Graham's dancers, like those trained in classical ballet, were constantly forced into painful and unnatural positions, which frequently resulted in chronic injuries. Erick came to feel that there there was something deeply flawed and perverse about any aesthetic that brutalized and damaged the bodies of dancers.

Graham is rightfully regarded and lauded as a revolutionary, as the most influential exemplar of an emergent modern dance, and is rightly praised, too, for developing a specifically American dance vocabulary in contradistinction to classical ballet. Ironically, however, with respect to the stress it put on her dancers' bodies, Graham's choreography was not a departure from the European tradition but an exacerbation of it. Notoriously, she once forced a dancer to hold a position that resulted in a broken back. She herself cultivated the autocratic allure of great

European choreographers for whom the body was an instrument not a vehicle, an instrument of flesh and bone strangely unconnected to the whole human person.

For too many of her dancers, like their counterparts in classical ballet, the body and mind were locked in a perpetual struggle that causes constant suffering—a suffering that can always be justified and dismissed in the name of art, and which too often became a perverted version of a sacrificial myth. In the case of classical dance, despite its own indisputable beauty and sublimity, such a myth has become a necessary creed. Graham's aesthetic, too, created, if not the ravishing illusion of grace afforded by classical ballet, then a kind of high drama, an agonistic spectacle often expressing intense struggle, a drama dependent to an uncomfortable degree on the more mundane reality of a sanctioned cruelty.

Erick sought an aesthetic responsive to the American ideal of freedom, an aesthetic unfolding without obstruction from within, and not enforced from without, which honored the dancer as much as the dance. A clear, open sense of space oriented to discovery rather than definition and a clear sense of place privileging the concrete and particular over the artificial and the abstract were necessary for the health of the human body, a whole body undivided either from the mind or from the heart, which is naturally, for man and woman, the measure of all things. For Erick, the alignment of spirit, breath, and body was a prerequisite for a clear, open relationship of the whole person, alert to discovery, to the exploration and understanding of places and spaces both inner and outer. It is entirely apt and unsurprising that one of Erick's first articulations of his dance aesthetic is a brief, typically laconic, manifesto called *The Body is a Clear Place*. He deemed it essential that man and woman accept, not recoil, from full embodiment, an acceptance that also involves the embrace of a world that is in no way alien to the body as a vehicle of the spirit.

Olson drew an analogy between the body and the house, both of which are human habitations. Olson wrote that consciousness should situate itself at the door of this house, ever alert from moment to moment to both what is being admitted into it and what is departing from it, undistracted by the evasions of the abstract and abstracted mind.

With respect to the temporal, for both Erick and Olson as well as for Williams —and as well, finally, for other artists and visionaries, both Eastern and Western, before them—attentiveness to the moment that is close to the quick of consciousness is paramount. Only the moment, the individual instant, opens out into and admits the true vastness not only of time but also of space.

For both Olson and Erick, poetry and dance are enactments of a consciousness hewing close to the always-ongoing moment of attention. Both dance and poetry allow the vast potential inhering within what Blake called "the pulsation of an artery" to be vitally actualized.

One of the first pieces of Erick's that I saw at the Joyce Theater was *Plains Daybreak*, which remains for me, if I had to choose, Erick's quintessential work. Its venue is the American West, which was Erick's place of origin. Its time is, of course, dawn, or rather the moment just before dawn. The curtain opens to reveal a number of figures wearing glorious animal masks created by Erick's longtime collaborator, the sculptor Ralph Dorazio. It is not quite true to say of this opening tableau that it reveals figures wearing masks; rather, it reveals and somehow realizes the emergence into being of these totemic animals themselves—animals no doubt akin to those with whom Native Americans and their shamans identified. Together, a tremendous sense of presence, and of making present, accrue to and emanate from these figures. At the same time, the masks they wear, as Erick was fully aware, are reminiscent of the origins of Greek theater in which mute, masked dancers—later to evolve into the choruses of Greek tragedy—ecstatically moved to sounds that seemed to spring from the original source of music itself.

Increasingly and gradually, light dawns on the plains, moving subtly through a variegated spectrum. As the first notes, or rather sounds, of a shimmering score begin to emerge, the animals, slowly at first and then more vigorously, begin to move. Their movements become freer, more ecstatic, the more that light floods the stage and the more the radiant strains of the score become prominent. The effect is somewhat like the crescendo of Ravel's *Bolero*, a crescendo in which not only music but the totemic animals and the increasing light that floods the stage participate. We are witnessing a tremendous dynamism arising from stillness as the subtlest traces of pre-dawn light burst into the clearness of Blake's "Glad Day." We are watching, it seems, the dancing of the beginning of the world. Olson quite beautifully referred to himself as "an archeologist of morning." In this dance, Erick's dancers, too, become, if not archeologists of morning, then ecstatic embodiments of it, reveling in the light of an always new day.

We remember that for Erick,

> If the dance is to be of excellence and vitality, and if it is to be a metaphor of our existence, then we have to consider what good existence is, or even what existence is, period. ...So my conclusion is if you want to arrive at quality—real intensity and real excitement in the art of dance—you have to look at real quality in existence.

It seems to me that Erick's work has an affinity, too, with that of Heidegger, for whom ontology and the realization of quality in existence was a primary concern. Heidegger's spiritual ancestors, like Olson's, stretch far back in time to the great pre-Socratic Greek philosophers.

For Heraclitus, who wrote in pithy, gnomic, now fragmentary aphorisms that are akin to the sutras of many Indian spiritual texts, it is paradoxically constant change and transformation in the form of fire that is the one unchanging first principle, a principle restated by Olson in the first line, nicely balanced by a medial slash, of his poem "The Kingfishers"—"What does not change / is the will to change." For Parmenides, however, Being itself was the primary principle. For countless philosophers, Eastern and Western, attempts to reconcile these two apparently contradictory principles—pure being and the ever-changing appearances of the phenomenal world—have been a constant preoccupation.

Heidegger was not interested in existence or being as mere lifeless abstractions but in the coming of things into the full radiance of their being. This requires, as for Hawkins, a kind of clearing, a sacred space or *temenos,* whether literal and physical, or a subtle space that art can open up in the heart, mind, and spirit. Heidegger makes clear in his work on aesthetics, in the extraordinary essays collected in his book *Poetry, Language, Thought,* that the role of the artist is to realize such clearings and the coming into presence of the things of this world that they make possible.

At the same time, for Heidegger, the coming into presence of things is always intimately related with their concealment and departure. Likewise in the tantric figure of the *Nataraj,* the dancing Lord Shiva, Shiva not only performs the functions of creation, maintenance, and destruction—assigned to Brahma, Vishnu, and Shiva respectively—but also of revelation and concealment. These latter two functions are not logical opposites but are dynamically interrelated, are constantly, simultaneously transpiring.

By extension—and here I am making explicit what Heidegger does not—presence is always related *not* to absence, which is a mere logical opposition to presence, nor to the void misconstrued as mere absence, but to what Buddhists call *emptiness*, which is the open space from which things arise into being and into which they subside. Just as writing on a page that is already full of print is unintelligible, thus requiring that one write on a blank page, so things that appear against a cluttered background, as Hawkins made clear, are unintelligible and never come into the fullness of the articulation of their being. Emptiness is analogous to the space between words on a page, the liminal space that, when focused upon, grants one access to the true nature of things.

All things subside into emptiness even as they arise from it. In the words of the *Heart Sutra*, a pithy précis of Mahayana Buddhism, "form is emptiness, emptiness is form." Similarly, for Hawkins, dance, the articulation of space by means of the body and its vocabulary of gestures, requires an uncluttered mind on the part of the choreographer, a sense of the body itself as a clear place on the part of the dancer, and a sense of space or place as an almost sacred clearing, a backdrop against which physical gestures can arise into clarity of articulation—and finally, a sense of all of these things as a totality, a wholeness that is reflected on every level.

One thing that all forms of art have in common is that they cannot rest in mere abstraction or play with sterile logical opposites that endlessly generate each other.

Rather, they unfold, make actual as articulated form, the very real energy of what was heretofore potential. All forms of art are the enactments, in more or less concrete ways, of this energy. They are vital, living enactments of the ongoing act of attention of Consciousness itself.

As I have drawn analogies above between the praxis of Hawkins and of several preeminent American poets, I wish belatedly to strike a kind of balance here by quoting what are among the most widely known lines of another great Anglophone modernist poet, a poet in this case not American but Irish. The following lines are the ecstatic conclusion of Yeats' great poem "Among School Children."

> Labour is blossoming or dancing where
> The body is not bruised to pleasure soul,
> Nor beauty born out of its own despair,
> Nor blear-eyed wisdom out of midnight oil.
> O chestnut-tree, great rooted blossomer,
> Are you the leaf, the blossom or the bole?
> O body swayed to music, O brightening glance,
> How can we know the dancer from the dance?

The labor referred to here is indifferently the physical effort of the dancer and the mental labor of the poet, whose respective art forms are drawn together by analogy. Some kind of labor, acknowledged in the stanza's first line, is a precondition for the ecstatic blossoming with which the rest of the stanza is concerned, and which celebrates a perhaps impossible-to-realize, ideal vision of art that is not merely sacrificial; an art in which the the pleasure of the soul does not come at the expense of or through the sacrifice of a bruised and damaged body; in which beauty is not necessarily a tragic beauty wrung out of its own despair; and in which wisdom is not only purchased by the sacrifice of youth to bleary-eyed old age.

The blossoming being described here is in no way forced but is as natural as the growth of that "great rooted blossomer," the fruit-bearing chestnut tree itself. The image of the tree in this poem, as elsewhere in Yeats' poetry, is symbolically the *axis mundi*, the macrocosmic world tree that yokes, in its upward thrust and its downward anchoring, the transcendent to the immanent. It cannot be accounted for by any enumeration of its parts—by leaf, blossom, or bole—but is an indissoluble whole, a living continuum.

Yeats would have known that his Romantic forebear Keats said of poems, in a letter to Charles Taylor, that "if Poetry comes not as naturally as the leaves to a tree it had better not come at all." He would also have known of Coleridge's concept of organic form, according to which, by analogy, poems, like living things, have a kind of inner telos to which, as they develop, there is a continual adjustment of part to whole and whole to part, a process that is finally and consummately realized in the finished poem, which, like a plant, embodies the whole history of its development.

A more radical analogy of Coleridge's organic form is suggested by holography. Each slightest segment of a holographic image contains the whole just as the whole contains each part. I have mentioned that for Whitman, each stage of the creative unfolding of consciousness, apart from pure Consciousness itself that pervades all, is contained by higher levels and contains lower ones, and that all thus are alike not only as being both container and contained, but as being fully pervaded by Consciousness, a boundless continuum in which all things participate. So, too, the the body of Yeats' dancer is one with the ecstatic continuum of the dance itself, a dance that is, by extension, like the dance of Lord Shiva, one with the play, the dance of Consciousness itself in which all things are drawn together in an ecstasy of continual consummation.

Though Erick did not share my interest in Romanticism or in Western poetry in general, and though he was influenced by Buddhism—specifically by Zen—rather than by Hinduism, it seems to me that he would have resonated or have felt himself in consonance with the notions that I have briefly touched upon above.

4.

Even during the period in which he was garnering respectful notices, Erick's company and my father seemed always to be fighting a rear-guard battle, seemed always to be on the brink of insolvency. This situation was exacerbated by certain of Erick's core principles, principles that were not negotiable. He insisted that his company dance only to live music, never to recordings, which added considerable expense to an already overly strained budget.

Erick viewed dance as a collaborative process, congruent with a "concept of totality" in which the bounds of the circumscribed ego were transcended. He commissioned scores by a number of composers, among whom were Virgil Thomson, Alan Hovhaness, Wallingford Riegger, Ross Lee Finney, Lou Harrison, Michio Mamiya, Lucia Dlugoszewski, and Ge Gan-Ru; and sets from Robert Motherwell, Helen Frankenthaler, Isamu Noguchi, and his long-time collaborator Ralph Dorazio, who, as I previously mentioned, fashioned the ravishing animal masks worn by Erick's dancers in *Plains Daybreak*.

Theater, dance, and music are perhaps the most inherently collaborative of art forms, whereas poetry as it has evolved in the West is perhaps the least. Although he was less engaged with poetry than with music and with the visual arts, Erick, as noted above, viewed dance as a "metaphor for our existence." Moreover, though in different ways, rhythm is an essential aspect not only of music and of poetry but of dance as well. Erick would have known too, as I have touched upon before, that in the work of the early Greek tragedians, music, poetry, and dance all played an essential role.

Erick composed a number of works that entailed discursive or narrative elements that reflected Erick's broad interest in myth and ritual; specifically, again, in classical, American Indian, and Japanese myth. Erick was a close friend of Joseph Campbell, whom he met as a young man, and was a particular admirer of his four-part magnum opus *The Masks of God*. One of Hawkins' late works in the mythic mode, *The Killer of Enemies: The Divine Hero*, seems in particular an homage to Campbell and to his first characteristic book, *The Hero with a Thousand Faces*.

The majority of Erick's mature works, however, were plotless. These works were often described by critics as abstract, a term that usefully suggests Erick's affinity with abstract expressionist painters, but which he disliked. Dance for him, as suggested above, was perhaps the least abstract, the most embodied of art forms.

As I continued to make my yearly pilgrimages to the Joyce Theater, I found myself over the years most drawn to these plotless works. They seemed to me to represent Erick's aesthetic in its purest, most distilled form. To borrow terms from Nietzsche's *The Birth of Tragedy*, I think that Erick's instinct as an artist—though it included the Dionysian, the erotic, and the ecstatic, particularly in late works in the mythic mode like *God, the Reveler*—was essentially Apollonian and contemplative, more concerned with the beautiful than with the sublime. His plotless dances in particular seemed, like Japanese rock gardens, to operate on the principle that less is more.

Among such works of Erick's that I most vividly recall are *Black Lake*, *Angels of the Inmost Heaven*, *Classic Kite Tails*, *New Moon*, and *Summer Clouds People*, which was dedicated to my parents. Alas, the specifics of these dances have faded from my memory. What remains is a sense of the numinous aura with which they seemed invested.

My first exposure to Erick and his work, which was less than auspicious, was a program in Carnegie Hall in 1975. Erick, who was at that point sixty-five, was still the lead dancer in many of his pieces, and he seemed to me sadly past his prime. The occasion felt celebratory but also a bit melancholy. One of the pieces he performed was *Hurrah!*, an idealized celebration of America's Independence Day, which was meant to end with the principal dancer ecstatically and triumphantly thrusting a phallic fist through the center of a straw hat, immediately after which the stage lights grow dark. On this occasion, however, the hat was recalcitrant, and Erick needed a second try to punch through it.

This first exposure to Erick's work inspired little interest in me. Several years later, however, in the late '70s, while living in an ashram in upstate New York, I began to trek down to New York City every year, making a pilgrimage to the Joyce Theater to watch one of Erick's programs, all of which included the premiere of a new dance as well as revivals of older ones. I began to feel a deep affinity for Erick's work, work that seemed to keep growing richer and freer. I loved the apparently easy yet intricately precise flow of his dancers' bodies—bodies that, due to Erick's care, were seldom subject to injury. I found myself more and more over time becoming a same-hearted viewer of Erick's work and began to experience something like same-hearted seeing.

Erick's work came to feel more realized as he grew older. His finest work, it seemed to me, spanned a period from the late 1960s, at which point he was sixty, to his death at the age of eighty-five in the early '90s.

5.

Erick extended to me a blanket invitation to visit him backstage after whatever performance at the Joyce I attended, and from there we habitually proceeded to a tiny studio apartment that he shared with his wife, Lucia Dlugoszewski, a brilliant, Pulitzer Prize-winning, avant-garde composer who provided, more than any other composer, the live music to which Erick's company danced.

Lucia was Erick's complementary opposite, his other half, just as he was hers. Whereas Erick tended to be laconic, even taciturn, Lucia was exuberant, garrulous, and above all uncensored. She was also completely devoted to Erick. She was known for sweeping down upon whatever unwary critic might be in attendance at any given performance, regaling him or her with her own breathless admiration for the piece that was being premiered, and cheerfully but forcefully suggesting that they share her appraisal.

Lucia, every bit as much as Erick, was a true original. Her endearing, sometimes exasperating manner tended to obscure the fact that she too had a first-class intellect. Before choosing to fully embrace her vocation, she had begun her adult life as a chemist. Early in her musical career, Lucia had produced large orchestral works. For one of these pieces, *Fire, Fragile, Flight,* she became the first woman to receive the prestigious Serge and Olga Koussevitsky Award. Virgil Thomson, one of Erick's musical collaborators, wrote that her music had

> great originality, beauty, and delicacy of sound ... ingenious with regard to instrumental virtuosities, and of unusually high level in its intellectual and poetic aspects.

The composer Ned Rorem wrote that she was one the five greatest living composers. Erick wrote to Northrop that more than anyone else Lucia "understood the the relationship between hearing and seeing," presumably between same-hearted listening and same-hearted seeing, one of my recurrent themes in this and the preceding essay.

At some point, a rare performance of one of Lucia's larger orchestral works took place in a theater on the upper West Side. I could in no way have anticipated my reaction to Lucia's work, to the entrancing risings and fallings of its unique, shimmering, lush textures of sound. Listening to it, one felt slightly airborne, as though drifting in and out of a radiant cumulus cloud.

Many of the instruments in the orchestra were invented by Lucia. Still others were repurposed, including a piano whose opened lid revealed strings pinched at various points by clothespins and muffled at other points by strategically placed wads of paper. Her orchestra included a particularly large brass section whose instruments were torqued and twisted into novel shapes that flashed and glowed, reflecting the light that shone upon them. The transporting delight imparted by this work was as much visual as aural, reflecting the fact that Lucia indeed understood the relationship between seeing and hearing.

It was clear that Erick and Lucia lived on almost nothing. Unlike Bill Maxwell, Erick had no charmed circle, no golden cenacle of admires. Nor did he consider dance a secular religion.

By the time I knew him, Erick's face had become noble and somewhat craggy with age. He remained very much the laconic Westerner. There was something, too, of the stoic about him. Our conversations did not have the same easy flow that characterized my meetings with Bill. Still, over the years, we became increasingly close. Erick, unlike Bill, not only asked to see copies of my work but read them, along with Lucia (always, he told me, out loud) with enthusiasm. He even remarked that he found my aesthetic somewhat similar to his own.

I suspect that Erick, like many bisexual men, was predominantly gay, which was, again, a kind of unspoken bond between us. Lucia, unlike Martha Graham, seemed to be genuinely untroubled about this. I suspect but have no way of knowing that Erick was conflicted about his sexuality and perhaps, given a kind of flinty taciturnity and streak of asceticism in his temperament, about intimate relationships in general. I suspect, again without knowing it, that his affairs were more often Platonic than sexual, and that some of those which he might have wished were sexual were sadly unreciprocated.

When Erick and my father were nearing eighty, they had strokes at around the same time. Erick made an almost full recovery. My father, alas, did not. During the five remaining years of his life, Erick created of some his most compelling and fully realized work. It was extraordinarily inspiring to see it.

Toward the end of his life, there began to be discussions about how best to preserve Erick's legacy after his death, which was no longer presumed to be far off. There were not sufficient funds to make more than a few tapes of his work, and it would take dancers thoroughly familiar with Erick's repertoire to keep his company viable. But as his company was always on the verge of insolvency even when he was alive, I think all concerned feared that the attempts to continue to perform his work after his death would confront perhaps insurmountable obstacles.

During this period, something again forcibly struck me, something which I had always felt but which was now coming into focus. I knew that dance notation is inadequate at best and is difficult to interpret even for those who are familiar with a choreographer's work. I began to confront a possibility that Erick, who was fundamentally a realist, also must have confronted: that it was possible that virtually nothing from the brilliant body of his work would outlast him, that it might all vanish like contrails in a summer sky. I began to ponder, again, what it must have been like to keep passionately, in the moment, creating work whose very nature was to be ephemeral, that might soon enough disappear as though it had never been created—and despite knowing this, to persevere and to lead a life of almost Franciscan poverty. I cannot imagine continuing to write without some expectation that my work will eventually be read. Erick seemed governed by a purity of intention that was in some way, though he was no saint, almost saintly.

One morning I awoke to find Erick's obituary on the front page of *The New York Times*. I knew it would give Lucia at least some measure of consolation that his death was afforded such pride of place.

I found myself, much to my surprise, weeping. I had not wept even after my father's death. I think that I was, at that moment, experiencing in a distilled way the purity of Erick's vocation. Again, he was no saint. But at the same time, he had stood for something irreplaceably valuable. Something indispensable.

A number of months after Erick's death, I wrote a brief elegy for him, just as I had written one for Bill. It is the shortest poem I have ever written, but something about its laconic condensation seems appropriate for Erick.

TILTED ARC

For Erick Hawkins

Your slightest gesture commands the space
That you inhabit, risky soul;
The rapt, impermanent edge of grace,
The impalpable paradigm you extol,
Is traced and retraced in the lambent air.
The mere civilians whom you enthrall
Are poised within a tilted arc
Describing that grand, eccentric sphere
From which you rise, and still arise
(For all your reverence for the ground)
And need not condescend to land.

For several years after Erick's death, Lucia poured her dauntless and indefatigable energies into keeping his company intact and afloat—with limited success. She even choreographed a few pieces of her own. When she died suddenly at the age of seventy-four, it came, given her seemingly inexhaustible energy, as a shock. Sadly, it took several days for her body to be discovered. Erick had left his estate to her, but she had left no will, which complicated attempts to properly preserve and archive their works. Lucia's music, set down in her own sometimes necessarily eccentric notation, analogous to the dance notation referred to above, seemed destined, too, to be almost entirely forgotten.

I am happy to report that my fears, and those of some others, have been to some degree unfounded. Due to the extraordinary devotion of a number of his dancers, The Erick Hawkins Dance Company under the leadership of Katherine Duke remains a fitfully going concern, periodically performing either entire dance works by Hawkins accompanied by Lucia's ground-breaking scores, or portions of them, though financial exigencies continue to be a pressing concern.

There has also been a resurgence of interest in Erick's dance technique as well as fresh explorations of Erick's place within the avant-garde milieu with respect to which he was both a participant and a dissenting voice. Fortunately, the musicologist Kate Doyle is currently engaged in organizing the archive of Lucia's work, which has found its way to the Library of Congress.

In yet another example of a series of the coincidences, or non-coincidences, that I have recounted in this text, in the early years of our current, rapidly changing century, I happened to be strolling by a Borders bookstore, once a leading bookseller that has now long since been displaced by Amazon. The now-defunct store in question was located near Columbus Circle in New York City. A poster strategically situated near a window caught my eye. It furnished the name and date of an event that was soon to be held there, a reading by the author, Renata Celichowska, of a recently published book, *The Erick Hawkins' Modern Dance Technique*.

I decided, on what felt like a whim, to attend.

As it turned out, I was impressed by the author's reading of the book and by the discussion that followed. I was even more impressed by its author, a vibrant, beautiful, and clearly highly intelligent and perceptive young woman two decades my junior.

After the reading, I introduced myself to Renata, who had long been a lead dancer in Erick's company, and mentioned that my father had been chairman of its board. Thus commenced what became, during my time in New York, a wonderful friendship. I learned from Renata, who was herself a talented choreographer, and who was at that time teaching at NYU, that my father was much loved and admired by all who were associated with Erick's company, and that he had taken a personal interest in the welfare, financial and otherwise, of many of its principal dancers.

This reconnection to my father was very meaningful to me. At the same time, I was introduced, through Renata, to a number of former dancers of Erick's company, who were impressive and admirable both as a group and as individuals, as well as to some of her friends in the contemporary world of modern dance.

Renata's painstakingly researched, concisely written book, reflecting her close association with its subject, has played a significant role in spearheading a resurgence of interest in Erick's dance technique.

Through Renata, I briefly met Laura Pettibone Wright, for many years a dancer with Erick's company and now a dance historiographer, who has used her intimate knowledge of Erick's dance notation to re-stage, in whole or in part, a number of Erick's works. Additionally, using an archive in the Library of Congress that now houses both Erick's and Lucia's papers, she is currently engaged writing a much-needed biography of Erick.

In a final coincidental twist, after I had finished this essay, I sent it to Renata, who in turn sent it to Laura, who then contacted me. She sent me a Powerpoint presentation on Erick's collaborations with various artists and composers. Through this wonderfully evocative presentation, I learned of one of the earliest works that Erick choreographed, *Ahab, The Fiery Hunt,* based, of course, on *Moby Dick*, and indicating a conscious affinity with Melville, of which I had been unaware. The scenario, or script, for the first version of this "play-dance" was written in 1946 by Robert Fitzgerald, whom Erick must have gotten to know when both were students of classics at Harvard. A revised script was written in 1947 by none other than Charles Olson. The Powerpoint presentation contains a facsimile of a letter by Olson to Erick. Thus Erick was connected to both Fitzgerald and Olson near the beginning of his career as a choreographer and their careers as poets.

~ Chapter 3 ~

Coda: The Unicorn and the Echo

In India, there is a term, *pandit*, that has no precise equivalent in English. The term is honorific. It refers primarily to learned teachers of various spiritual traditions who have through practice assimilated the wisdom of those traditions. Included among such figures are academic teachers of these traditions, with respect to whom the assimilation through practice of their wisdom is considered a boon, not, as in the West, a detriment to the proper objectivity of the scholar. In sum, pandits embody what they teach and impart to their students not only intellectual knowledge but the wisdom of their attainment.

The term *pandit* also quite specifically pertains to masters of classical music who strive to pass on that mastery to their students. The great musician, too, is seen as an embodiment of a kind of wisdom and discipline analogous to that attained by spiritual masters. Thus the term *pandit* refers to the teaching of both metaphysics and of aesthetics.

Until recently in India, the relationship between masters of classical music and their student/disciples was extraordinarily intense. Typically the student, having received teachings from the master, spent long hours every day practicing and studying. The student lived near or with the master. His or her long apprenticeship entailed a total immersion in music. What the teacher imparted to the student involved, to quote from Olson, "more than the merely technical." It involved a kind of silent transmission through which the student absorbed the master's deep intuitive experience of music. Most students, like most disciples of gurus, have been unable to fully receive and assimilate this transmission and all that it implies. Their education, however, has not been in vain. They attain an extraordinarily high level of technical proficiency. Again, however, only a precious few can absorb all that the master has offered and then make it, in effect, their own, themselves becoming masters, attaining not merely technical proficiency but the freedom and invention of genius. The kind of all-consuming artistic apprenticeship I am describing has been dying out in India and has never really existed with a similar intensity in the West. Nevertheless, it occurs to me that the mentors whom I have described in the foregoing pages were all, to an unusual degree, the embodiments of the wisdom of the disciplines they sought to master, and that they were thus analogous to pandits. I consider myself lucky, to whatever degree and however briefly, to have been in the presence of such figures.

It seems to me, also, that if I had to choose one word that best describes the relationship between student and pandit, a word that encapsulates, as well, my attitude toward the figures whom I have discussed in this essay, it would be *reverence,* a term often employed in a religious or spiritual context that can equally be employed in a secular one.

Of course irreverence, humor, irony, and yes, an exuberant, even a scabrous vulgarity, and certainly the acerbic edge of satire, have their proper or improper place in any healthy culture, as do play and playfulness. All are indispensable *rasas,* vital aesthetic flavors or colorations. But reverence, too, is indispensable, is an attitude that binds us not only to figures we admire in the present but to that which connects them and us to what is vitally alive in the past, which in turn keeps alive in us another aesthetic emotion, *wonder,* a wonder that can connote, as well, a sense of awe and of the sublime.

Reverence and wonder are emotions that suggest our response to the vastness and mystery of the universe that we inhabit, as we inhabit our bodies and the buildings in which we dwell, and suggest as well another term, *humility,* not as a sense of abasement but as a kind of right relationship to a cosmos, "of which," to quote the words of Wallace Stevens, "we are too distantly a part." A culture that has lost a capacity for reverence, humility, wonder, and awe is a culture that had lost its way; is a field in which cynicism, decadence, and a smug knowingness begin to prosper; and in which these other, indispensable human qualities come to seem naive and déclassé.

In thinking about wisdom, the wisdom embodied by the figures to whom I have attempted to pay respect in this essay, a poem by the great Polish poet and political dissident Czeslaw Milosz, who spent much of his life writing in the shadow of a totalitarian regime, comes to mind. He celebrates, in his poem "Incantation," the friendship, the filial bond, between "Philo-Sophia" and poetry.

Philos is a Greek root meaning to love or to have an affinity for. The word *sophia,* too, is embedded in the word *philosophy.* It is another Greek term that connotes a kind of numinous wisdom. It is personified, as employed by several Hellenistic philosophers, as feminine, as the mother or bride of the divine word or logos.

The "reason" to which Milosz refers reverently at the outset of his poem is not syllogistic reason. Nor does he have truck with the irrational, which can be even more destructive than an unbridled rationality. Milosz is referring to reason raised to a higher power, to reason that entails a love of wisdom.

When such wisdom is allied with poetry, something miraculous takes place. It is role of the poet, and of all artists, to keep what Wallace Stevens calls the light of the imagination alive even in the darkest of times, even amid political regimes in which the arts are subverted, devalued, and debased.

Poetry when allied with wisdom sees the potential that remains to be realized even in the face of the destructively actual, counsels hope instead of despair. It binds together same-hearted readers, same-hearted listeners, and same-hearted seers into cells of celebration and resistance. Reason, which when deployed judiciously is in itself a good, when allied with poetry, or with dance and music, blossoms into a wisdom that is beyond but includes reason, becomes a kind of miraculous good news, a gospel, "brought to the mountains by a unicorn and an echo," by the seeming chimeras of poetry, a good news that is both ancient and ever new, that keeps both wonder and reverence for indispensable human values alive.

An incantation is a summoning into being, into presence, of that which is intoned. Dance, music, poetry, and the visual and plastic arts, architecture, all are embodiments and expressions of the logos considered *not* as analogous to any merely linguistic word, but to that deep resonance or vibration of a non-localized Consciousness that makes present and articulates that which it calls forth.

INCANTATION

Human reason is beautiful and invincible.
No bars, no barbed wire, no pulping of books,
No sentence of banishment can prevail against it.
It establishes the universal ideas in language,
And guides our hand so we write Truth and Justice
With capital letters, lie and oppression with small.
It puts what should be above things as they are,
Is an enemy of despair and a friend of hope.
It does not know Jew from Greek or slave from master.
Giving us the estate of the world to manage,
It saves austere and transparent phrases
From the filthy discord of tortured words.
It says that everything is new under the sun,
Opens the congealed fist of the past.
Beautiful and very young are Philo-Sophia
And poetry, her ally in the service of the good.
As late as yesterday Nature celebrated their birth.
The news was brought to the mountains by a unicorn and an echo.
Their friendship will be glorious, their time has no limit.
Their enemies have delivered themselves to destruction.

II. COMING TO TERMS WITH ROBERT LOWELL

~ CHAPTER 4 ~

DISOWNING LOWELL

1.

Robert Lowell was a WASP. So, too, am I. Lowell came from a prominent family. Let me stipulate from the outset: so, too, do I.

Or perhaps it would be more accurate to say that I come from a once-prominent family. Its roots can be traced back on both sides to the Mayflower. And yet Lowell's work, alone among that of the poets I have chosen to discuss here or elsewhere, did not and in some ways still does not inspire in me any sense of elective affinity. On the contrary, I was initially repelled, or rather both repelled and fascinated, by his poems. I felt no inclination to be a same-hearted reader of Lowell, to intuit whatever it was that was the murky wellspring of his strangely dark poetic productions. I was perversely happy instead to be a stone-hearted reader of Lowell's work. And yet the very intensity of my ambivalence toward his poetry was indicative of a kind of involuntary affinity. His writings laid claim on me—a kind of ancestral claim, perhaps, rather than a spiritual one.

For any poet, those poets from whatever epoch with whom one feels a kinship quite naturally become allies, facilitators of one's own artistic development, or in some cases influences to be constructively overcome. I think it is equally though less obviously true that those poets—and I am referring here to poets of genuine stature —whom one strongly and instinctively reacts against likewise contribute to one's evolving sense of one's self-definition as a poet. They, too, can become unlikely allies.

My initial feeling of revulsion and ambivalence toward, and my ultimate coming to terms with Robert Lowell's poetry, which will be my subject in this and the ensuing essays, is intimately bound up with our somewhat shared provenance.

There are striking similarities in particular between my mother's background and that of Lowell. They were of the same generation, born, in fact, one year apart, and they grew up in the same milieu, to which they reacted in ways both similar and significantly dissimilar.

Lowell's childhood was solitary and grim. He was the scion of two once-illustrious families that, if his mother and father were any indication, seemed to be in decline. Lowell reserved a special contempt for his parents, and for his father in particular, about whom he would later write several quite astonishingly cruel poems. He was considerably more charitable to members of his mother's clan, whose surname, Winslow, had almost as much cachet as did his own.

Lowell never felt at home in the Boston Brahmin society into which he was born. Nor did he seem particularly inclined to condemn it. He regarded himself and was regarded by others as a misfit. At St. Marks, the prep school which he attended, he was nicknamed Cal, short for both Caliban and Caligula, a sobriquet that was quite spectacularly revealing.

Lowell as Caliban was deemed ungainly, uncouth, unlike his more prototypically WASP classmates who, schooled in the social graces, were taught to value athleticism over scholarship, and for whom the proverbial gentleman's C, far from being a mark of opprobrium, was a badge of membership in the club. Schools like St. Marks prided themselves in churning out leaders—doers rather than thinkers. They were a breeding ground for a WASP elite whose manifest destiny, it was assumed, was to ascend to positions of eminence in the corporate and financial world, or in a few top law firms, or in government.

Lowell, large, shambling, and habitually unkempt, conspicuously lacking both social graces and athletic prowess who, when not writing an endlessly long, metrically unvarying poem on the Crusades, spent a considerable amount of time with his nose stuck in books, betrayed no signs of incipient leadership. For his part, he found his classmates, with a few crucial exceptions who would become lifelong friends, a dull and homogenous lot.

Cal as Caligula was a somewhat more alarming figure. Not only was Lowell, who if not athletic was both large and physically powerful, prone to capricious and unpredictable outbursts of violence, but he also had what would turn out to be a lifelong fascination with tyrants and despots, a fascination that he did nothing at that time to conceal. Caligula and Nero hardly exemplified the myth or ideal of democratic or republican leadership that schools like St. Mark's embraced.

Lowell himself seems to have been a subject more of bemused, condescending fascination than of outright contempt. He was tolerated rather than ostracized. He felt trapped in a narrow, confining, familial milieu that he saw no viable prospect of escaping. When he attended Harvard, as had generation after generation of Lowells, his existential discomfort only increased. After having been forced to perform menial chores, Lowell/Caliban was refused membership in the *Advocate,* Harvard's redoubtable literary rag, whose ramshackle premises was a kind of clubhouse for those marginal young souls brave enough to dabble their toes in the streams of Parnassus. Lowell was too marginal even for the marginal.

Eventually, his behavior grew increasingly erratic until finally a kind of crisis or breaking point occurred. During an argument with his father over the suitability, or unsuitability, of a woman who was fleetingly his fiancée, he knocked the slight and frail Commodore Lowell out cold with a single deftly delivered blow to the head, an episode that became for Lowell a kind of primal act in his myth of himself. His easy dispatching of his father rendered the old man even more pitiable and contemptible in his son's eyes.

Lowell's parents, fearful for their safety, seriously considered institutionalizing him but instead, in what seems a providential act, remanded him to the care of Merrill Moore, a socially prominent Boston psychiatrist. Aside from his professional duties, Moore devoted himself to what would become a lifelong vocation or avocation—the production of an endless series of sonnets. Moore felt considerable affection for his new charge. The bond between Moore and Lowell was strengthened by their mutual interest in poetry. Lowell had never before experienced this kind of respect and understanding. Moore told Lowell's parents, on scant evidence, that their son was a genius, and that henceforth they should not expect Lowell to conform to them. Rather, it was their responsibility to adapt to his moods and needs.

Moore, who was originally a Southerner and who knew, from his youth, a number of prominent fellow Southern poets, suggested that Lowell take a year off from Harvard and study informally with his friend, the poet Allen Tate, at Vanderbilt University in Tennessee. His parents were no doubt relieved at the prospect of enjoying a respite from their dangerously unruly son. Lowell's departure from Harvard was deemed scandalous enough to merit mention in *The Boston Globe*.

Tate, John Crowe Ransom, and at that time Robert Penn Warren were prominent members of the so-called Fugitive school of poetry, a genteel Southern outpost of what was then called the New Criticism. They shared a kind of nostalgia for the old, agrarian, aristocratic South, similar in kind to the strain of reactionary nostalgia for a supposedly more civilized and aristocratic society in Eliot and especially in Yeats, though not to the histrionics of the more unhinged Pound. As a political program, their ideas were not only eminently impractical but willfully impervious to the fact that the agrarian, aristocratic South that they longed to resurrect was intimately bound up with and dependent upon the institution of slavery. And yet despite their eccentricities and blind spots, they were passionate, devoted, and above all serious students and practitioners of poetry. They were doubtless intrigued by the prospect of having a potential Yankee convert in their midst.

Upon arriving in Tennessee, Lowell, with a more than typical lack of social grace as well as with the presumption of one who unconsciously arrogated to himself the prerogatives of an unquestioned aristocrat, asked if he could become, for a nominal fee, a boarder in the Tates' home, whereupon Tate declined, jokingly suggesting that Lowell pitch a tent on their lawn. Lowell headed to Sears Roebuck, bought a tent, and indeed planted himself in the Tates' backyard. He would become something of a boarder after all. The Tates must have been thoroughly nonplussed by the takeover of part of their property by the uncouth young Yankee. In any event, they seem not to have had the heart to expel him. Lowell lived in the tent for two months before finding more conventional accommodations elsewhere.

When Tate and Ransom were offered tenured teaching positions at Kenyon College in Ohio, Lowell followed them and enrolled as a student there. Lowell's years at Kenyon were a blessed interlude. Ransom, with an extraordinary generosity born of his affection for Lowell, became more than a mentor to him. Ransom wrote in a letter to Tate about the paternal feelings he harbored for Lowell, in whom he, like Merrill Moore, recognized the makings of a major poet.

Lowell graduated from Kenyon with highest honors in the classics. He returned home with a distinct trace of a Southern accent, which all assumed would be a fleeting affectation but which remained throughout the rest of his life a characteristic feature of his speech. Perhaps this new accent served notice that, though returning to the fold, Lowell would be in but not entirely of it.

In his mid-twenties, Lowell married the novelist Jean Stafford. To his credit, he was always drawn to women of formidable intellect, most of them writers. The marriage, however, was a disaster. Lowell's outbursts of violence, no doubt in part fueled by his as yet undiagnosed mania, increased in frequency and intensity, and were terrifying to Stafford, who was likewise unstable, and who tried to match Lowell's physical violence with a caustically witty disdain. This situation, of course, proved untenable. Lowell twice struck Stafford, breaking her nose both times. His physical abuse of his wife became the first in a series of seemingly unforgivable actions that were prompted by his mania. Not long into their marriage, as a result of a car crash that occurred while Lowell was speeding, Stafford's once extraordinarily beautiful face was permanently disfigured. Lowell did not seem loath to add injury to insult.

No longer ensconced in the protective enclave of Kenyon, Lowell, psychically at sea, converted with a manic fervor to Catholicism. He immersed himself in Aquinas, Augustine, and more contemporary Catholic theologians. He subjected both himself and Stafford to a kind of improvised monastic discipline.

During a brief sojourn in the South, this time as invited guests of the Tates, Lowell and Stafford experienced a kind of respite, a return to a happier time. Lowell's first characteristic poems began to emerge. Out of the ferment of this period, Lowell's first collection, *Land of Unlikeness*, later thoroughly revised and published as *Lord Weary's Castle*, was born. The latter, upon its publication, was met with a frenzy of New Critical approbation. Lowell was off and running as a poet.

Soon enough Lowell returned to New England, where he and Stafford would once again feel unsettled, unmoored, at loose ends. A key episode of this epoch of Lowell's life was his decision as a conscientious objector not to fight in the Second World War. He sent a rather bizarre personal letter to President Roosevelt in which the grandiose authority he imagined his family name conferred on him is embarrassingly apparent.

> Dear Mr. President,
>
> I very much regret that I must refuse the opportunity you offer me in your communication of Aug 6, 1938, for service in the Armed Forces.
>
> ...You will understand how painful it is for an American whose family traditions, like your own, have always found their fulfillment in maintaining, through responsible participation in the civil and military services, our country's freedom and honor.
>
> I have the honor, sir, to inscribe
myself with sincerity loyalty and
respect, your fellow citizen,
>
> Robert Traill Spence Lowell, Jr.

Lowell assumes here a quite astonishing intimacy where none in fact existed. His letter sounds as though he is responding to an invitation from one grandee to another to participate in a polo match—though it was, of course, the draft board, not the president, who had sent Lowell his draft notice. The accompanying one-page declaration delineating the reason for his decision is even more turgid and pompous than this cover note. It makes clear that Lowell is not a pacifist but is objecting to what he anticipates will be a plan to completely annihilate Japan and Germany. There is some rich irony in Cal/Caliban, lover of despots, prone to personal outbursts of violence, occasional and casual batterer of his wife, casting himself—heroically, of course—as a conscientious objector.

Meanwhile, the perceived indignities to which Lowell subjected—despite his high regard for his last name—his poor, crimped, pitiful parents continued unabated. First there was the mythical felling of the father, then the scandalous retreat from Harvard to Tennessee, then upon his return, his adoption of a Southern accent, and then, one would have thought to top it all off, his conversion from Protestantism to Catholicism, the creed of Boston's immigrant hordes. Lowell's refusal to fight in the war, occasioning several ignominious months in jail, was yet another provocation.

The considerable power and prestige of those with a prototypically WASP background was fully intact during Lowell's youth and remained intact throughout much of his life. Being a Lowell had undeniable cultural cachet. Lowell, while excoriating his nuclear family, nonetheless, it seemed to me as young man, quite consciously took advantage of the power his name conferred upon him. Lowell's blanket condemnation of his native Boston in his first book as the "Whore of Babylon" included not only those of his own class but its immigrant population as well. By including his relatives in his indictment, he augmented the power conferred on him by his name, and what was regarded as his moral authority, far more effectively than would have been the case had he graciously passed over them in silence.

2.

My mother was the granddaughter of Nelson Aldrich, who was for many years the powerful Republican Senate majority leader from Rhode Island. As a result of assiduously promoting the interests of big money while in the Senate, he amassed a small fortune and built a grand mansion in Warwick, Rhode Island. He also developed a keen interest in the visual arts, which inspired a similar passion in his daughter Abby, who married John Rockefeller Jr. This passion played a part in her co-founding the Museum of Modern Art in New York City.

In some ways, my mother's trajectory in her early years ran parallel to Lowell's. Her father, who was the scion of a prominent New England family that had lost most of its money, seeking to make his own way in the world, had headed West, where by his early thirties, after beginning as a laborer, he had become vice-president of the Great Western Sugar Company in Denver. He died suddenly of the Spanish Flu when my mother was four, and so her mother—who, if her letters are any indication, both loved and admired her husband—now consigned to what would become a feeling of permanent bereavement, returned to Boston from Colorado.

Like Lowell, my mother felt herself to be a misfit in Boston society. She came to loathe the parochial, anti-Semitic, and anti-immigrant WASP enclave in which she grew up. She never felt comfortable with her peers at Milton Academy. Despite having a remarkable, disqualifying ineptitude in math, she, too, by dint of privilege and the fact that the entire lineage of the male side of her family had attended Harvard, was admitted to Radcliffe where, unlike Lowell, she spent all of only one deeply unhappy year, during which she continued to live at home.

Since childhood, my mother had been repeatedly told that she looked exotic, a reference to her atypically dark complexion that was not meant as a compliment. Throughout her life, in what now would doubtless be considered a kind of inverse racism, my mother felt a particular affinity for Jews, particularly for Jewish intellectuals, and for Italians. As not only a misfit but a rebellious devotee of the unconventional, she also felt a special affinity for artists of all kinds, especially for writers, while feeling increasing contempt for "people like us," a tribe of which she refused to consider herself a member. She even succumbed to the satanic charm of

Roosevelt and become a registered Democrat, a then unheard-of defection, the ultimate betrayal of her class and caste.

Finally, in an act which must have required considerable courage, she fled Boston and moved to New York, where she took classes at George Balanchine's School of American Ballet. For a considerable fee, students of various ages were allowed to observe and to minimally participate in classes there, including a few presided over by the master himself, Balanchine. Our mother later regaled my three sisters and me with stories of legendary figures like Maria Tallchief, a Native American who became Balanchine's New York City Ballet's most prominent prima ballerina.

There is not much I know about my mother's time in New York during the ten years or so between her arrival there and her first meeting with my father. I do know that she spent two of those years, when she would have been in her mid-to-late-twenties, not in New York but in Europe where, as a volunteer with the Red Cross, she had been sent in the immediate aftermath of the Second World War. Her primary responsibility was simply to interact compassionately with young soldiers who were beginning their transition home, many of whom were ravaged by what we now call PTSD.

It appears that my mother had no serious affairs or even flirtations with any of these soldiers, perhaps surprisingly since she was described by those who knew her at the time as being quite beautiful, although, again, in an unconventional way. Instead, judging by her letters home during this period, her feelings toward the soldiers with whom she interacted was primarily maternal, which was probably what many of them most needed at the time. Still farther away from Boston and its dreary social climate than she had been in New York, I think that for the first and sadly for the last time in her life, she felt genuinely useful.

My mother's marriage brought to an end what seems to have been a relatively idyllic period in her life, reactivating demons that had been, at least for a time, held at bay. She was consumed by anxiety about how to comport herself as a wife and later as a mother, two roles for which, although she had longed to assume them, she somehow felt radically unprepared.

My father spent his undergraduate years at Harvard where he evinced an unusual gift for mathematics and developed a love of classical music, particularly of Mozart and Haydn, as well as a refined aesthetic sense in general. He graduated Phi Beta Kappa, near the top of his class. He secretly wanted to be an architect, an altogether too-marginal and artistic vocation, and felt duty bound to join what was a long lineage of lawyers on his father's side of the family. My paternal grandfather, whom my father adored, was the founder of what became a prominent law firm in New York. He was apparently an affable and much-loved man. There is some indication that he suffered periodic depressions. Sadly, he died of a heart attack at the age of fifty-six when my father was in his last year at Harvard.

In order not to ruin his memories of that august institution, my father attended Yale Law School, after which, unsurprisingly, he became a lawyer, a profession which, as he had feared, he found deeply uncongenial. Less than a year later, my father suffered the first of what would become for him recurrent depressions. Though this necessarily secret affliction was a hindrance to his career, my father rose from junior staffer to eventually becoming, for many years, the executive director of the Council on Foreign Relations in New York, a foreign policy think-tank that was the genteel epicenter of the foreign policy establishment.

For a man of his time and place, he was remarkably devoid of prejudice. He was also relatively without affectation. These qualities endeared him to my mother. They were married in their mid-thirties and had a long, difficult, turbulent, yet fundamentally loving marriage. The difficulty sprang not only from my mother's insecurities about her new role but also from my father's depressions and from the central, tragic event in my mother's life, the aforementioned death of her father, with whom by all accounts she had an extraordinarily strong bond. As a result, my mother went through life fearing that some disaster was imminently in the offing. My father's depressions were a kind of existential threat to her, fueling her lifelong fear of abandonment. This fear led to a state of constant anxious paralysis. Though my mother had a number of artistic gifts, she cultivated none of them.

My parents spent their summers in a house my father had purchased three years prior to meeting my mother, on the north shore of Long Island, on its so-called Gold Coast, a bastion of the Mid-Atlantic rather than New England strain of the WASP elite. My father and a number of his relatives had summered not far from this house. Again, with her typical reverse snobbery, my mother felt contempt, in principle, for her WASP neighbors on Long Island and refused to have anything to do with them, which resulted not only in tension with my father, whose friends she refused to countenance, but in the isolating of our whole family to a quite extraordinary degree.

Though my mother loathed the snobbery of her relatives in Boston, she was at the same time not-quite-secretly proud of her pedigree, occasionally or more than occasionally affording glimpses of a kind of ambivalence that was all the more powerful for being mostly kept hidden. I remember, for example, her low opinion of people who used the word *drapes* instead of *curtains*, one of many such linguistic sins, identifying those who used them as déclassé, most of which I have by now, thankfully, forgotten. My mother, in short, was not only a reverse snob but also a snob of a more conventional stripe. I felt, and to some degree incorporated as my own, my mother's ambivalence. Her subliminal message to me and to my three sisters was that we were better than/worse than others. On one side of the equation, she harbored quite grandiose ambitions for her children, that they excel in some unconventional sphere like the arts, while on the other she feared that we would prove somehow defective, unable, as she felt unable, to flourish.

Of my life I will have relatively little to say. After having myself spent my quota of miserable years at prep school where I, too, felt out of place, I matriculated at Harvard in 1970. Though not egregiously unqualified, there is little doubt that without what is now euphemistically referred to as legacy admissions, I would have attended college elsewhere. I felt disaffected and aimless during my freshman year, largely as a result the lingering effect of trauma undergone at various previous junctures of my life. A few months into my sophomore year, I suffered a severe depression and was remanded to the compound, or compounds, of an eccentric and abusive psychiatrist, first in Florida, then in Pennsylvania.

After about nine months, my depression suddenly lifted. I spent the brief interim before I returned to Harvard at my parents' apartment in New York City. One afternoon, I pulled a book from a bookshelf. The book was *Ariel* by Sylvia Plath. I have no idea how it got there. Neither of my parents were aficionados of poetry. After perusing this book with some fascination for about an hour, I sat down and wrote four poems. By the time I was finished, I had an odd, unaccountable yet preternaturally clear sense that my vocation in life was to be a poet, a sense which from that time forward has never wavered.

Rather than advertising my provenance at Harvard, where I soon found myself repeating my sophomore year, I kept it a closely guarded secret. In part this was to avoid being stereotyped. I had no inclination to be regarded as a dull, conventional beneficiary of privilege. At the same time, I was somehow keenly aware that being a WASP was a currency that was beginning to lose its value, and that it would continue to depreciate—quite rapidly, as it turned out—over time. Attempts to trade on my name, or in my case on my grandmother's maiden name, Aldrich, would not have been as valuable as such commerce had been for Lowell. I felt, moreover, a kind of ethical compunction about engaging in such trade. My life in large part became an exercise in detaching myself from whatever advantages and disadvantages my background had conferred on me.

Perhaps I felt something akin to what citizens of a colonial power must feel when they sense that their power is beginning to wane. Though still the beneficiaries of privilege, the more sensitive among them are perhaps prone to begin to question the legitimacy of a system from which they still benefit. Perhaps the most sensitive begin to feel something like shame over their unearned prerogatives, and to seek out arenas in which, stripped (as much as possible) of the inherited mantle of privilege, they will be judged on the basis of their own proven merit or the lack of it.

Finally, I had known since the age of twelve that I was queer, which then, of course, was a highly pejorative term. The term *gay* had not yet, to my knowledge, been coined. This was yet another secret to be kept mostly hidden. My vague, implausible, grandiose childhood dream of being a senator had long ago shaded into a vaguer, only slightly more plausible dream of being a great writer.

3.

Before plunging into an evaluation of Lowell's poetry, I want to make clear that the judgements I pronounce in this first of my two chapters on Lowell are all reflective of my view of him—as I shall occasionally, indeed perhaps too often, remind the reader—when I was a young man, an assessment that did not begin to change until after my second episode of depression in my early thirties. The nature of that change and of my more mature assessment of Lowell are the subjects of the final essay in this book.

In my prior, brief account of Lowell's coming of age, I took leave of him at the time when he was engaged in writing *Lord Weary's Castle*, a book that made a considerable impression on me when I first read it. Indeed, upon its initial appearance it had an overwhelming impact upon critics. New Criticism, which was in its heyday when the book was published, was characterized by a fastidious regard for nothing but the poem itself, which it insisted on viewing as a self-sufficient and hopefully internally consistent whole, and which had a particular fondness for teasing out the multiple connotations of rhetorical tropes, a process that typically yielded up a rich harvest of ambiguity. The poet/critic William Empson's *Seven Types of Ambiguity* is at once the most extreme and most brilliant exemplar of this tendency. In its fascination with the unpacking of local tropes, New Criticism sometimes came close to swerving away from its primary mandate, which was to examine the contribution of a poem's parts to the achievement of a self-enclosed whole. Unsurprisingly, New Criticism tended to valorize poems that exhibited strong closure and to devalue poems in so-called open forms that did not conclusively circle back on themselves.

Lowell's generation was rife with poet/critics who followed in the footsteps of T. S. Eliot, among them Lowell's mentor at Kenyon, John Crowe Ransom; Lowell's friend Randall Jarrell; and on the West Coast, Yvor Winters, whose stringent critiques of his fellow poets could be as chilly as his last name. John Berryman was not only a poet/critic but also a poet/scholar. He labored for years at the self-appointed task of emending the text of *King Lear*, work that, though it was left incomplete, was and in fact still is well-regarded by scholars. In general, the poets of Lowell's generation were expected to be highly learned and to be engaged with criticism as well as with poetry. Lowell himself, though he wrote relatively little criticism, was omnivorously if somewhat eccentrically well-read.

The early critics of Lowell's poems, many themselves New Critics, were so overwhelmed by the rhetorical force of *Lord Weary's Castle* that they failed to register the conspicuous fact that Lowell's poems, though satisfyingly formal, and though certainly exhibiting strong closure, were completely devoid of ambiguity of any kind. Instead, they are painted with broad, bold, sometimes powerful, sometimes grotesque, and in general quite simple strokes. Catholicism, with its appealing certainties, seemed to have granted Lowell a respite from ambivalence and from the burden of being a Lowell.

And yet Lowell's poems in *Lord Weary's Castle* in no way reflect the ethos or the sensibility of Catholicism. When Lowell got religion, he essentially got the religion of his Puritan forebears, for whom the psychotic revenge fantasy of the *Book of Revelation* was the primary—and the Old Testament prophets the secondary—text, and who managed to bypass the good news of the Gospels almost entirely. In poem after poem in *Lord Weary's Castle*, Christ is never the living Christ of the Gospels, nor a loving intercessor, nor a bestower of grace. Instead, Lowell is obsessed with Christ's crucified body, the mangled object of a violence that was always fascinating to him. This fascination with violence becomes a kind of dark celebration of the lurid and the extreme. Christ also appears in poem after poem as the unforgiving judge of the *Book of Revelation*.

Lowell's poems scarcely make even a pretext of dressing up in Catholic garb. When they do make such an attempt, it is almost always perfunctory and unconvincing, as in the obligatory nod to the Virgin Mary in "Our Lady of Walsingham," the penultimate section of "The Quaker Graveyard in Nantucket," which seems merely to be slipped into the poem as a sop to Catholic orthodoxy. Lowell's prophetic wrath is trained upon Boston, now regarded as a fallen and unregenerate Babylon. His stance is robustly condemnatory. And yet precisely what is being judged, beyond his hometown, is unclear. At times it seems that the whole unregenerate, fallen world is being indicted.

Lowell's imagination was stirred far more by his Puritan forebears—figures whom he assiduously studied and to whom he repeatedly returned—than by Emerson, Thoreau, or Whitman. Indeed, the spirituality of many of the figures associated with what used to be called the American Renaissance, and particularly that of Whitman, was antithetical to the ethos of Lowell's beloved Puritans. For Lowell, it was almost as though the so-called American Renaissance had never taken place, and that the figures who were associated with it, with the exception of Hawthorne and Melville, were too negligible to be taken into account.

"The Quaker Graveyard in Nantucket," the centerpiece of *Lord Weary's Castle*, is nothing if not a bravura rhetorical performance, in part Old Testament jeremiad, in part a battle hymn that is nominally an indictment of the Second World War, in part a linguistic tour de force that solipsistically worships at the altar of its own power.

The poem is an ambitious attempt to write a classical elegy. It is modeled after Milton's "Lycidas," with Hopkins' "Wreck of the Deutschland" and Crane's "Voyages" lurking in its rhetorical background. It is written in a sinewy and powerful iambic pentameter that occasionally, strategically, admits lines of a lesser length. It indulges and sometimes over-indulges in a plethora of sound effects, glorying in both clipped and harsh consonants ("A brackish reach of shoal off Madaket...") and more fulsome vowels. The poem is an extravagant, irresistible soundscape.

Lowell serves notice of his rhetorical prowess at the poem's outset with a depiction of the drowned body of his cousin Warren Winslow, the elegy's nominal subject. The whole first section, whose opening lines I quote below, has a mesmerizing and compelling rhythm, deploying iambic lines of varying lengths and irregular end rhymes to great effect.

> A brackish reach of shoal off Madaket—
> The sea was still breaking violently and night
> Had steamed into our North Atlantic Fleet,
> When the drowned sailor clutched the drag-net. Light
> Flashed from his matted head and marble feet,
> He grappled at the net
> With the coiled, hurdling muscles of his thighs:
> The corpse was bloodless, a botch of reds and whites,
> Its open, staring eyes
> Were lusterless dead-lights
> Or cabin-windows on a stranded hulk
> Heavy with sand.

This passage, like the body of a serpent, sinuously uncoils. The depiction of Winslow, light flashing from his head and feet, grappling at the net with the "coiled, hurdling muscles of his thighs," suggests not so much a dead body as a sprinter poised at the starting blocks before the sound of the gun; the effect is one of tremendous energy held in reserve, which is the effect of the first section of the poem as a whole. When we remind ourselves that Winslow's body is in fact dead, it comes as something of a surprise. The rhetoric of the poem's succeeding sections is likewise powerful but is denser and more agglutinated. The tongue of the mind must work strenuously to pronounce them.

The central, obsessive motif of "The Quaker Graveyard" is Melville's tale of the hunting of the white whale in *Moby Dick*. The unnamed vessel whose sinking resulted in the death of Winslow is metaphorically identified with the Pequod in *Moby Dick*. World War Two, which Lowell opposed, is thus linked to a daemonic quest. As the poem unfolds, the Pequod's hunt for the white whale is referenced in each of its numbered sections with the exception of the aforementioned, gratuitously inserted "Our Lady of Walsingham."

I have noted Lowell's echoing of his Puritan forebears' obsession with what I have called the psychotic revenge fantasy of the *Book of Revelation*. Ahab's quest is in part just such a psychotic revenge fantasy, one that becomes disastrously real due to the visionary force of his obsessive imagination. His constant, insisted-upon rage is ultimately and blasphemously directed not only against the whale but against creation itself.

Despite the ubiquity of the references to *Moby Dick* in "The Quaker Graveyard," it is difficult to identify their place in the symbolic economy of the poem. The status of the whale in particular is ambiguous. I am not referring to New Critical ambiguity here but to something more like its mundane cousin, simple confusion. What precisely is meant in the poem's third section by "IS, the whited monster"? Is the word "IS" an echo of Jehovah's reference to himself in Exodus as " I am That I am?" Is the whale, like Christ, a sacrificial victim, somehow aligned with God? Or is the "IS" a reference to the unredeemed created-ness, the brute actuality of the fallen world? Lowell, a novice in his handling of Biblical symbolism, tends to deploy its repertoire of tropes as stock figures. The whale as "monster" is symbolically Leviathan, a name that crops up not only in "The Quaker Graveyard" but also quite frequently elsewhere in *Lord Weary's Castle*. Leviathan, along with his terrestrial confrere the Behemoth, represents Satan's presence in the world. And yet, confusingly, the mission of the Pequod, far from involving an extirpation of evil, is itself an expression of it. The poem's fourth section is almost entirely taken up with an indictment of the foolishness of Ahab's mission, which leads to the Pequod's ultimate "packing off to hell."

"The Quaker Graveyard," like *Moby Dick*, ultimately drives toward its central event, the killing of the whale.

> ...Sailor, will your sword
> Whistle and fall and sink into the fat?
> In the great ash-pit of Jehoshaphat
> The bones cry for the blood of the white whale,
> The fat flukes arch and whack about its ears,
> The death-lance churns into the sanctuary, tears
> The gun-blue swingle, heaving like a flail,
> And hacks the coiling life out: it works and drags
> And rips the sperm-whale's midriff into rags,
> Gobbets of blubber spill to wind and weather,
> ...

This depiction, or verbal re-enactment, of a paroxysm of violence is, as a piece of writing, extraordinarily vivid and alive, particularly in the cumulative force of its verbs, which are, with the exception of two participles, all active: whistle, fall, sink, cry, arch, whack, churns, tears, heaving, hacks, coiling, works, drags, rips, spill... Likewise, the passage is dense with sound effects of all kinds—alliteration, consonance, assonance, rhyme, and off-rhyme—whose thickness and density reflect the physicality of the violence that is taking place.

The final section of the poem, which follows the weak, rote tribute to Our Lady, the Virgin Mary, is an anti-climax. It ends with yet another Old Testament reference, this time to the rainbow that appears in Genesis after the flood as a sign of the reaffirmation of God's new covenant with man: "The Lord survives the rainbow of His will." This proposition, which has the tone of a ringing summary and conclusion, seems at best a truism and at worst meaningless. The more one ponders it, the emptier, the more a resounding space-filler it comes to seem.

The symbolic armature of the poem, however one interprets it, ultimately seems beside the point. The real thrust of the poem lies in its glorying in its own sheer linguistic power and ultimately in its fascination with power, specifically violent power, itself. Power, particularly capricious, arbitrary power, had always had a hold on Lowell's imagination. The nominally Catholic but in fact Puritan ethos of Lowell's religious phase gave him a new vocabulary with which to elevate his sense of personal grievance and disaffection, to grant it a kind of universal sanction. Ironically, the poem, which clearly intends, at least in part, to be a condemnation of the violence of the Second World War, is despite itself a kind ode to wrath.

Apart from the "The Quaker Graveyard," the most lauded poem in *Lord Weary's Castle* was "Colloquy in Black Rock." Its setting is the church of Hungarian immigrant workmen who were building ships for the war effort in the Connecticut coastal town in which Lowell and Stafford were living at the time of its composition. That the poem is another bravura exercise in violent rhetoric is evident in its opening stanzas.

> Here the jack-hammer jabs into the ocean;
> My heart, you race and stagger and demand
> More blood-gangs for your nigger-brass percussions,
> Till I, the stunned machine of your devotion,
> Clanging upon this cymbal of a hand,
> Am rattled screw and footloose. All discussions
>
> End in the mud-flat detritus of death.
> My heart beat faster, faster. In Black Mud
> Hungarian mechanics give their blood
> For the martyre Stephen who was stoned to death.

The fact that the third line of the poem contains a word that even at the time of its writing was recognized as offensive is not all that feels off-key here. The words "mud" and "blood" continue to echo throughout the poem, which is a kind of brutal imagining on the part of the poet of violent martyrdom, of a fate which, one senses, he more than half wishes might be his own. This wish seems to necessitate the mortification of a world whose body, in order to be regenerated, must be broken down into undifferentiated, primal slime, a moil of muck and blood.

Typically, the poem's last stanza is crammed with obligatory references to Christ, to his crucified body, to his walking, here grotesquely covered with mud, on water, and finally to the stock image of Christ as a kingfisher who, in the poem's last words "dives on you in fire," an evocation of Pentecost that somehow brings to mind instead the suicide missions of Japanese dive bombers toward the end of the Second World War. If the poem is a testament at all, it is a testament to a pathology, to the exhilarating manic state that seems to have engendered it.

The most unequivocally successful poem in *Lord Weary's Castle* is one whose subject allows Lowell to dispense with any pretense of Catholicism. I am speaking of "Mr. Edwards and the Spider," a powerful poetic recasting of Jonathan Edwards' "Sinners in the Hands of an Angry God," a quintessential hell-fire and brimstone sermon, which lingers lovingly over the agonizing fate of souls in hell, and whose primary text, again, is *The Book of Revelation*. Melville, in a rhetorical tour de force in chapters 7 through 9 of *Moby Dick*, gives voice to a sermon that the lay pastor Mapple delivers in a chapel for whalers that both parodies and at the same time projects the power of this kind of apocalyptic language.

Edwards' writing, unlike that of most of his Puritan confreres, had a kind of literary and visionary vividness, and Lowell, who would write on Edwards often, felt for him a kind of literary and ancestral affinity. "Mr. Edwards and the Spider" is completely without Melville's irony. It takes its subject entirely seriously. I will cite here the first and fourth of the poem's five stanzas.

> What are we in the hands of the great God?
> It was in vain you set up thorn and briar
>   In battle array against the fire
>   And treason crackling in your blood;
>   For the wild thorns grow tame
> And will do nothing to oppose the flame;
> Your lacerations tell the losing game
> You play against a sickness past your cure.
> How will the hands be strong? How will the heart endure?
> ...
>
> On Windsor Marsh, I saw the spider die
> When thrown into the bowels of fierce fire:
>   There's no long struggle, no desire
>   To get up on its feet and fly —
>   It stretches out its feet
> And dies. This is the sinner's last retreat;
> Yes, and no strength exerted on the heat
> Then sinews the abolished will, when sick
> And full of burning, it will whistle on a brick.

The poem stresses the Puritans' fatalistic sense that no struggle, no exertion of our own can stave off whatever fate is predestined for us on the day of judgement. It quite intricately stretches out its metrical feet, though fortunately it does not die. It reflects not only the Puritan obsession with the damned but also, I suspect, the terrifying fires of full-blown mania in which the will of the sufferer is likewise extirpated, in which all autonomy, all sense of personal responsibility is incinerated, in which one knows not what one does.

After *Lord Weary's Castle*, Lowell published a much briefer volume, *The Mills of the Kavanaughs*, a strangely listless performance. One senses the manic high of Lowell's infatuation with Catholicism wearing off. The title poem is notable primarily as Lowell's only extended foray into narrative verse. Its thinly veiled subject is Lowell's violent marriage to Jean Stafford. The poem's speaker is the aggrieved female partner, now widowed. Perhaps it is in some measure an attempt on Lowell's part to see his violence through another's eyes and thereby to appraise it and himself with some degree of objectivity. And yet once again, the poem's rhetoric is both violent and lurid, at times almost hallucinatory, and torturously baroque, as though anticipating or recalling Lowell's as yet undiagnosed experience of manic psychosis. Lowell never manages to break out of the circle of his self-obsession, never succeeds in bringing either of the poem's protagonists to life, to render them convincingly as plausible, autonomous characters.

Lowell's next book, *Life Studies*, written after his infatuation with Catholicism had long since passed, was a radical break from his previously published work. No American book of poetry published during my lifetime has received such an ecstatic reception. *Life Studies* was heralded as revolutionary, as opening up the exploration of new, more distinctly personal terrain for poetry. This new mode was soon dubbed "confessional," a so-called school that I will explore at some length later in the essay following this one.

Lowell had long and surprisingly been an admirer of William Carlos Williams —so much so that had he not gone to Kenyon and fallen under the influence of Tate and Ransom, he claims that he might have earlier experimented with a more informal, and at the same time more accessible, style. At some point in the mid-fifties, Lowell gave a joint reading with Allen Ginsberg, in which his dense, marmoreal lyrics were thoroughly upstaged by Ginsberg's recitation of "Howl." To write poems whose immediate, visceral impact would move a potential audience as "Howl" did, Lowell realized that he would have to discover both a new subject and a new style.

Lowell had also long been an intense reader of prose fiction, which was the subject of one of the classes he taught at Harvard. He felt an affinity with French novelists and with Flaubert in particular. Lowell's interest in fiction was one catalyst for his search for some new poetic way forward. His new subject, in part an old subject handled differently, would be a species of memoir dense with novelistic detail.

To a remarkable degree, *Life Studies* flouted New Critical nostrums and norms. Its poems are not self-enclosed artifacts but rather are episodic, each poem forming tentative connections to others. Including Lowell's first forays into free verse, the poems in *Life Studies* abjure the strong closure of his earlier work in favor of a suggestive open-endedness. Above all, any pretense to the impersonality enjoined by Eliot, later to become an almost unquestioned tenet of New Critical dogma, was swept aside.

And yet no howls of New Critical outrage were occasioned by *Life Studies*. It seemed that Lowell, in real time, was forging the taste by which his work would be received. It was as though the triumphal chariot of Lowell's poetry was leading the way, with critics happy to make whatever adjustments were required to move comfortably in its wake. The lure of the apparently revolutionary is difficult to resist. Even critics of settled opinion are loath to chastise what seems destined to become the next "new thing."

My awareness of the reputation of *Life Studies* preceded my first reading of it. My reaction to it was to feel thoroughly underwhelmed.

The second of the book's four sections is Lowell's prose memoir, "91 Revere Street." It was inspired, as was often the case with Lowell, by the work of a colleague; in this case, Elizabeth Bishop. Her story "In The Village" had a powerful impact on Lowell. It recounts, from the point of view of the poet as a child, her mother's terrifying descent into madness—and thus to her lifelong institutionalization and the child's abandonment to her own meager devices. The story is stark, bare, stripped-down, almost itself a prose poem, one with a kind of visionary intensity. Its central symbol, echoing throughout the story, is the scream of her mother as she is being led away to a mental hospital for the last time. Its subject, though intensely personal, never seems merely personal and becomes an evocation of the universal human experience of existential and metaphysical dread. Nowhere in the story is it explicitly suggested that we are reading a memoir.

The prose of Lowell's memoir, by comparison, feels as listless and enervated as the familial cast of characters, most in some way or another eccentric, to whom it introduces us. It also presents to us Bobby (Lowell as a child), who does not seem notably more interesting or prepossessing than others of his clan. I confess that I have never managed to get more than ten or fifteen pages into this piece, a piece that makes me feel as if I am trapped in a claustrophobic drawing room with someone else's boring relatives.

I found a number of poems in *Life Studies* as dispiriting as "91 Revere Street." Some, including the generally lauded "My Last Afternoon With Uncle Devereux Winslow,"—rare because of its relatively affectionate account of the impending death of a beloved uncle—began as prose pieces, which Lowell then arbitrarily chopped up into free verse. This poem and others similarly reconstituted from prose never achieve the fluency of effective free verse. Even those poems in *Life Studies* originally written in free verse seldom attain such fluency.

Though Lowell claimed that his chief influence, other than Bishop and Tate, was William Carlos Williams, even in *Life Studies* and afterwards in *For The Union Dead*, he continued to write in form as well as to produce poems like "Man and Wife" that are hybrids of formal and free verse. Later, in the case of his unrhymed sonnets, he would write in the semblance of form. Only his last book, *Day by Day,* was written entirely in free verse, and though it has many virtues, for the most part its poems, unlike those of Williams, feel arbitrarily enjambed and randomly divided into stanzas.

I want to make clear here, again, that I am recounting my initial and highly prejudicial reaction as a very young man to *Life Studies*. The modest or somewhat more than modest virtue of some of these poems was then lost on me. Their world felt to me claustrophobic, circumscribed, parochial, and pinched. I resented the presumption that I would find the world depicted in *Life Studies*, which seemed to me to lack the rhetorical power of *Lord Weary's Castle*, inherently interesting.

But my principal objection, an ethical one, to these poems was that they did not, as they had not in *Lord Weary's Castle*, direct their anger toward the depredations of Lowell's class, which I knew, partly from my first-hand experience at prep school and partly from the testimony of my mother, to be, at its worst, viciously racist and intellectually vacuous, stifled and stifling, self-satisfied and inbred. In *Life Studies*, Lowell's anger is most obsessively trained upon his overwhelmed and overmatched parents. Yet again, a kind of bullying violence is evident in these poems, particularly in his poems about his father. They seemed to me to have a cold, reptilian cruelty, which I quite simply found repellent. Repellent and somehow almost unforgivable. Not content to have knocked out his father once, Lowell returns to this primal scene repeatedly in poems written after his hapless parent's death. The first such posthumous re-enactment occurs in the poem "Rebellion" in *Lord Weary's Castle*.

> There was rebellion, father, when the mock
> French windows slammed and you hove backward, rammed
> Into your heirlooms, screens, a glass-cased clock,
> The highboy quaking to its toes. You damned
> My arm that cast your house upon your head
> And broke the chimney flintlock on your skull.

What is perhaps most disturbing about "Rebellion" is Lowell's obvious relish in and his loving contemplation of the detailed particulars of his memory of this scene. The poem seems to exhibit something like the relish that a violent psychopath might feel in mentally re-enacting the scrupulously, minutely remembered details of some atrocity—and this in a book, *Lord Weary's Castle*, that adopts a stance of high-handed condemnation both of the corrupted world in general and of the poor, contemptible souls who live and move and have their being within it.

In the poems "Commander Lowell" and "Terminal Days at Beverly Farms," Lowell lands less direct but far more telling blows upon his father. Both works evince toward the old man something like complete contempt. He is damned as pitifully ineffectual, too pathetic to move comfortably even among members of his own class, who feel nothing but a baffled condescension toward him.

These poems, on the other hand, are anything but ineffectual. They hold his father up—in what is again a kind of lurid spectacle—to the finest, most exquisitely calibrated ridicule. The last few stanzas of "Terminal Days at Beverly Farms" are a case in point.

> Father had had two coronaries.
> He still treasured underhand economies,
> but his best friend was a little black *Chevie*,
> garaged like a sacrificial steer
> with gilded hooves,
> yet sensationally sober,
> and with less side than an old dancing pump.
> The local dealer, a "buccaneer,"
> had been paid a "king's ransom"
> to quickly deliver a car without chrome.
>
> Each morning at eight-thirty,
> inattentive and beaming,
> loaded with his "calc" and "trig" books,
> his clipper ship statistics,
> and his ivory slide rule,
> father stole off with the *Chevie*
> to loaf in the Maritime Museum at Salem.
> He called the curator
> "the commander of the Swiss Navy."
>
> Father's death was abrupt and unprotesting.
> His vision was still twenty-twenty.
> After a morning of anxious, repetitive smiling,
> his last words to mother were:
> "I feel awful."

I have mentioned that *Life Studies* is essentially an episodic memoir in verse. Apart from those instances in which the chief interest is in the writing or in the historical or literary significance of the writer, the more interesting examples of this hothouse genre are rife with intimate details to which our natural response is a kind of guilty pleasure. *Life Studies* manages to be both finely written and luridly anecdotal. Here, as is often uncomfortably the case in some memoirs, the most ethically challenged of genres, violence is done to figures who can no longer fight back or speak for themselves.

4.

By the time I left Harvard, I had added additional charges to the already lengthy bill of indictments I had drawn up against both Lowell and his poetry. I have always found the Puritanism of my distant forebears singularly unappealing. The Puritans' fascination with the *Book of Revelation* and its fixation on final things, and in particular on the ultimate disposition of the soul, the horrific either/or of salvation or damnation, led in turn, it seemed to me, to a kind of sickness of the spirit, to an obsession not only with the status of one's own soul, to a dreadful yet always inconclusive seeking out of signs as to whether it was regenerate or unregenerate, but also to an even more unfortunate, judgmental obsession with the status of the souls of others. Who were among the regenerate and thus admitted to the church, and who were among the reprobate and thus excluded from it? Though there was no definitive test, no real way to make such a determination, nonetheless, as a practical matter, such judgements were routinely made. Likewise, again, there was no definitive way of knowing the status of one's soul. One's conviction that one was among the elect could very well be the work of the devil. Dread, a pervasive ontological uncertainty, as well as a kind of sickness and paralysis of spirit, was endemic to the radical Protestantism of the Puritans, for whom introspection could be as much a form of self-torture as of self-knowledge. That same self-torture, projected outward, led to atrocities like the Salem witch trials.

Nonetheless, what a high opinion the ragtag group of Puritan nonconformists held of themselves! Grandiosity characterizes their self-conception. Once again, in their view, God had elected the Puritans his "chosen people," who were to be a "New Israel," the typological fulfillment of their Old Testament forebears. They were to become, in John Winthrop's now hackneyed phrase, a "City upon a Hill," a beacon to all other nations. Roger Williams—from whom I am happy to admit I am descended—was having none of this. According to him, God had had only one chosen people, the Israelites in the Old Testament. He warned that his fellow Puritans' self-election as a New Israel was a dangerously self-serving delusion, that the apparatus of the state would come itself to be seen as the guarantor of the New Israel, and thus would be prone to the self-righteous exercise of arbitrary and despotic power. Even as the Puritan enterprise was plagued by doubt and dread, it was also paradoxically characterized by the rigid self-certainty typical of extremists of all kinds.

In Lowell's early poetry, self-certainty and grandiosity generally trump doubt and self-questioning. During his religious phase, as I have attempted to make clear, Lowell was a Puritan through and through, but even after that phase had passed, an obsessive concern with self remained, a concern that we as readers are expected, for no good reason, to share. Lowell's grandiosity was largely a result of the manic phase of his bipolar disorder, and his own sickness and paralysis of spirit—so brilliantly anatomized in poems like "Skunk Hour"—of its depressive phase. Both were biologically driven, but even during his periods of relative mental stability, Lowell intensely identified with his Puritan forebears.

Lowell was a product of the New Critical strictures against which he only partly rebelled. These strictures involved a particular dislike not only of Whitman and Emerson but of the great English Romantic poets who were their precursors, poets whom I particularly revered in my youth, and whom I still revere. With respect to the imagination, Blake and Coleridge, each in his own way, clearly regarded the muse of memory as antithetical to what Blake called the "Poetic Genius." In a ringing passage from his short epic *Milton*, Blake declares:

> I come in Self-annihilation & the grandeur of Inspiration;
> To cast off Rational Demonstration by Faith in the Saviour,
> To cast off the rotten rags of Memory by Inspiration;

For Blake, our ordinary sensory experience deludes us by trapping us in a world in which the rigid coordinates of time and space are supreme, and in which we consider not only our senses but our inner experience of the world as copies of a reality external to us. Moreover, we seldom attend to the present moment. Thus, the pictures we form of reality are already, by the time we examine them, faded, in the past tense. The commonsense view is that our senses' relation to the world is essentially passive. For Blake, to the contrary, the senses, when renovated by the poetic genius, are active, alive, and constitute what they experience; are capable of grasping infinity in a grain of sand and eternity in each present moment, in "the pulsation of an artery," thus freeing the poetic seer from the fixed coordinates of time and space mentioned above as well as from the notion of a supposedly stable, external reality that can simply be copied by the senses. Our commonsense picturing of reality is unfortunate enough, but memory, which consists of a storehouse of further degraded and even less reliable pictures, copies of delusory copies, is at yet a further remove from the the vision of the prophetic seer. It consists not merely of rags but of "rotten rags"—rags that it is the function of the poetic genius to incinerate.

Coleridge held a similar view of the imagination. He famously distinguished between the primary and secondary imagination, and between these and "fancy." In his *Biographia Literaria*, he states that the primary imagination is "a repetition in the finite mind of the eternal act of creation in the infinite I AM." The secondary imagination actively translates these passively received intimations of the divine into poetic form. In so doing, it makes use of what Coleridge calls the "esemplastic" power of the imagination, a power which "dissolves, diffuses, dissipates" our habitual mental picture of a frozen and fixed world in order to recreate it in the language of poetry, an act that is aligned with the creative act of the divine. The esemplastic power struggles "to idealize and to unify. It is essentially vital even as all objects (as objects) are essentially dead." Coleridge distinguishes this power from "fancy," which has "no other counters to play with, but fixities and definites," and which receives its materials ready-made from memory and from the law of association.

It seemed to me as a young man that Coleridge would have considered Lowell's poetry from *Life Studies* onward as works of fancy rather than of imagination, and that Blake would have regarded them as tricked out in the "rotten rags of memory." Lowell's poems in *Life Studies* and *For The Union Dead* seemed to me to be drawn in associative clusters from the storehouse of memory. I imagined that to my adopted mentors they would have seemed pictures of pictures, degraded copies of copies. They did not seem to generate, unlike the imagination, anything genuinely new, nor, in R. P. Blackmur's phrase, "to add to the stock of available reality."

In all of these and cognate Romantic views of the imagination, it is essentially seen as an active power. I have mentioned the power and relative frequency of verbs in *Lord Weary's Castle*. In subsequent books, however, the balance of lexical power increasingly shifts, one symptom of which is Lowell's stylistic quirk or tic of having a flotilla of three adjectives preceding nouns that are fixed or slow moving enough to be so accompanied. Adjectives, compared to nouns and verbs, are relatively interchangeable, and so their overuse encourages the kind of endless tinkering and revision to which Lowell fell prey.

The essentially static quality of much of Lowell's poetry subsequent to *Lord Weary's Castle* is evident in his sonnet series *History*. Reading the book is like taking a guided tour through a fusty portrait gallery in some English manor house—or should one prefer a more gothic analogy, it is like being trapped in a narrow, interminably long, basement corridor in a funeral home. The corridor is full of strangely small and confining coffins, each of which is open, providing a view of the garishly made-up faces of the embalmed deceased.

The poems in *History* are arranged in simple chronological order, the kind of chronology that Lowell, who had no gift for narrative and who never attempted a sustained narrative poem after the failure of *The Mills of the Kavanaughs*, often self-servingly mischaracterized as a "plot." In his "Afterthought" in *Notebook 1967-68*, the first of his books of sonnets, later revised, repurposed, re-gifted, and redistributed in several subsequent volumes of sonnets, including *History*, Lowell writes: "Accident threw up subjects, and the plot swallowed them." But the purely accidental and contingent, like entries in a diary, or jottings in a notebook, do not constitute a plot in any conventional sense.

Similarly, no attempt is made to discover any kind of dialectical dynamism or any dynamism at all in the unfolding of history. Lowell seems implicitly to subscribe to a naïve version of the "Great Man" theory of history. He is not only drawing from the storehouse of his own memories but at a still further remove, of memories of reading about historical figures. Lowell seems to regard history itself as a storehouse of collective memories or agreed-upon facts that has simply been added to with the ineluctable passage of time. Lowell plunders this storehouse, or warehouse, for static portraits of historical figures that are then shoddily framed by his tentative unrhymed sonnets. Once again, or so it seemed to me, we are receiving pictures of pictures, copies of copies.

5.

Lowell, having exhausted his stock of historical figures, having in effect caught up to the present, turned to transcribing, still in unrhymed sonnets, poems that chronicle his participation in the anti-war movement of the mid- to late-sixties. Finally, Lowell turned, in the same unrhymed sonnets, from matters political, reverting in *For Lizzie and Harriet* and *The Dolphin* to by now familiar, familial ground and to transcribing more or less literally the somewhat chaotic events of his inner and outer lives.

A scandal broke out regarding the matter of poetry-as-transcription when Lowell incorporated reworked versions of letters from his wife into those portions of *The Dolphin* that are a poetic chronicle of their divorce, a divorce that was occasioned by what proved to be no mere fleeting, manic infatuation and indiscretion but a fateful and disastrously disruptive attraction to the beautiful and intellectually formidable Lady Caroline Blackwood, a talented novelist and heiress to the Guinness fortune, who was to become Lowell's third wife.

Elizabeth Bishop wrote to him of these poems, after having said that "it is hell to do so":

> The first one, page 10, is so shocking—well, I don't know what to say. And page 47 ... and a few after that. One can use one's life as material— one does, anyway—but these letters—aren't you violating a trust? IF you were given permission—IF you hadn't changed them ... etc. But art just isn't worth that much.

Lowell and Bishop had met when they were both young poets and had felt instantly drawn to one another; in Lowell's case so much so that he later wrote to her, with a touching cluelessness, that his greatest regret in life was that he had not married her. Typically, in an era in which female poets often were regarded by their male peers with a kind of polite condescension, Lowell early recognized Bishop's poetry as at least the equal of his own. For her part, Bishop exempted Lowell from her characteristic, occasionally chilly reserve. Their warmth of feeling for each other and respect for each others' poetry is evident in their decades-long epistolary exchanges, most of which are now preserved in the volume *Words in Air*.

And yet their poetry had little in common. They used "life as material" in very different ways. Bishop wrote poems, always formally elegant, in which the details of her personal history are sublimated and covert; whereas in Lowell those details and the feelings associated with them are often foregrounded, and the forms in which his poems are cast can at times seem eccentric, makeshift, and ramshackle. Nonetheless, in their letters, Bishop and Lowell continually extol each other's work, and their reciprocal admiration, repeatedly affirmed, clearly mutually bolstered their morale.

In this context, Bishop's unprecedented reprimand is particularly telling. Bishop, who was, of course, close to Hardwick as well as to Lowell, must have found Lowell's abandonment of her a terrible betrayal; she clearly regarded not only Lowell's inclusion of passages of Hardwick's letters but his changing of them a gratuitous and unconscionable compounding of that betrayal. Bishop's objection is, of course, a moral and ethical one, similar in kind to my revulsion toward a number of Lowell's earlier poems, chiefly those about his parents in *Life Studies*. Given the high value that both Bishop and Lowell placed on art and their shared consciousness of the stringent and sometimes self-sacrificial dedication required in the pursuit of it, her statement that "art just isn't worth that much" is a particularly powerful indictment.

Parenthetically, when Bishop wrote in the same letter "first, please do believe I think *The Dolphin* is magnificent poetry," she was, in accordance with her usual, benign solicitousness toward Lowell's poetry, being somewhat disingenuous. In fact, as it is clear from comments made to others, she had considerable aesthetic as well as moral reservations about *The Dolphin* in particular and about Lowell's sonnets in general.

In the title poem of *The Dolphin*, one of the finest of Lowell's sonnets, he acknowledges that the book is "half fiction," and both proleptically anticipates and concurs with Bishop's indictment:

> I have sat and listened to too many
> words of the collaborating muse,
> and plotted perhaps too freely with my life,
> not avoiding injury to others,
> not avoiding injury to myself—

> to ask compassion ...

> my eyes have seen what my hand did.

In a phrase elided above, Lowell refers to his poetry as an "eelnet made by man for the eel fighting," a phrase that conflates phallic sexuality with violence, as though his poetry attempts but fails to contain the upheavals caused by a mania that entraps him in a cycle of destructive sexual excitement and self-lacerating regret. There is a hint, too, that Lady Blackwood is in some sense the net that has snared him. Blackwood is, of course, the dolphin of the poem's title, and Lowell the eel, and both are instances of the aquatic and sub-aquatic tropes that recur throughout Lowell's poetry, and that are perhaps emissaries from the turbulent and elemental realm of the overweening unconscious.

The poem's final line has an extraordinary, almost Biblical, resonance. It is as though Lowell's mania has caused him to be a passive, helpless witness of his unregenerate, ungovernable impulses. It was his hand, of course, that felled his own father and twice broke his first wife's nose. That hand, too, was too often an organ of a forbidden sexual intimacy. And it was Lowell's hand, finally, that wrote his poems, some of which he knew to have transgressed not only the bounds of propriety but also of simple decency, but which he nonetheless, to his repeated remorse, felt helplessly impelled to write.

Later, and particularly in his final volume, *Day by Day,* this tone of retrospective regret, which includes many genuinely confessional passages—in which Lowell repeatedly acknowledges harm done to others and tentatively seeks forgiveness—comes to predominate, and a touching, elegiac tenderness trumps rhetorical violence done either to himself or to others. As it is intimately bound up with my mature reappraisal of Lowell's work, I have deferred an extended discussion of *Day by Day* to the final essay in this volume.

6.

Lowell's *almost* endless series of sonnets wound up comprising, unfortunately, a disproportionately large chunk of his *Selected Poems.* They seemed to me as a young man, and largely still do, to be wrong-headed in conception and uncertain in execution, and to have a kind of rote, repetitive, moribund quality. To the extent that they live at all, they live in fits and starts. They seldom carry a single impulse, a single imaginative or rhetorical charge, from beginning to end. If Lowell's depiction of Warren Winslow's dead body in "The Quaker Graveyard in Nantucket" was powerfully and strangely dynamic, suggesting the coiled body of a sprinter just before the start of a race, many of his sonnets seem scarcely to make it out of the blocks. They seem, at times, to dither, unable to make up their minds. Finally, they have nothing of the logical architectonics that typically structure the sonnet. They do not even bother themselves with rhyming.

Lowell's sonnets were among the poems that he endlessly, obsessively revised. It seemed to me that the impulse to revise such poems arose from their lack of any intrinsic, imaginative impulse, any tropism toward imaginative coherence. They have the merely associative and anecdotal structure—or lack of structure—that characterizes what Coleridge calls poems of fancy. No clear criteria exist by which to judge any one version more successful than any other. And yet paradoxically but understandably, it was this very lack of criteria that led to Lowell's constant fiddling with these poems and to revisions that only served to exacerbate their general enervation.

Lowell's poetry from *Life Studies* on, it seemed to me, called almost exclusively upon the muse of memory. That Lowell was defensive about this aspect of his poetic stance is reflected in his remarkable last poem, "Epilogue," in which he longs to create something "imagined, not recalled." Later in the poem, he asks the rhetorical question: "Why not say what happened?" Though "Epilogue" is touching, it seemed to me as young man that Lowell too easily absolved himself. Lacking the enlivening power of esemplastic imagination, he regards even human beings as mere passing, eventually lifeless facts.

In response to Lowell's question "Why not say what happened?" one might, I thought, reply with another question, "*Why* say what happened?" Much of the force of "Epilogue" arises from what one feels is the poet's recognition that poetry needs to do more than merely record—like journalism or like an unimaginative version of history—what happens. Even the historian selectively deploys his material, giving versions of events that fit and reinforce a given narrative or point of view. There is something, it seemed to me, in the imagination, including in Lowell's imagination, that hungers for more than mere mimetic copies, whether provided to us by our senses or by memory—copies that are always unreliable and degraded—of a reality which we sadly presume to be external to us.

I must stress again that I have been discussing in this, the first essay of this section of this book, my reaction as a young man to Lowell. I eventually came to see my own early blanket condemnation of Lowell's work, from the rhetorically charged, if disturbing, poems of *Lord Weary's Castle*, to the more relaxed, autobiographical mode of most of his work from *Life Studies* onward, to be itself partial, parochial, and one-sided.

Later, I began to be more sensitive to the considerable pathos of Lowell's episodic autobiography in verse. Of course, even the remembered and recalled, in Lowell's more successful works, far from being antithetical to the imagination, are themselves reimagined, as all memories, as we now know, are to some degree reimagined and are sometimes entirely products of the imagination.

Finally, perhaps the most telling cause of my aversion to Lowell as a young man involved a factor of which I was not fully conscious. As I mentioned, I had gone through a harrowing, terrifying, and protracted episode of depression before returning to Harvard. I was, of course, thoroughly familiar with Lowell's multiple breakdowns and hospitalizations. Would I share not only Lowell's WASP provenance but his benighted and devastating fate as well? Lowell was, at this fundamental level, a figure with whom I very much did not want identify.

~ CHAPTER 5 ~

INTERLUDE: HEARING CONFESSION

1.

I confess, unsurprisingly, that as a young man I felt considerable resistance to and qualms about not only Lowell in particular but also about the confessional school of poetry in general. Some of the poems written under its banner, as I will make clear, I found persuasive, seductive, and even beautiful. But fundamentally I did not wish to make the merely personal vicissitudes of my life my subject. My early guides in these matters were Wallace Stevens, Bishop, Blake, and Whitman, who for all of his inclusiveness and apparent frankness had almost nothing at all to say about the details of his personal life. Indeed, he very effectively and cagily managed to bar all access to such details.

The first use of the word *confession* with respect to this newly emergent poetic mode appears in the critic M. L. Rosenthal's perceptive and prescient review of Lowell's *Life Studies*. Rosenthal notes that Lowell's poems "remove the barriers of reticence" and that, stripping away the distancing mask of an impersonal persona, the speaker of Lowell's poems "is unequivocally himself." He remarks that "it is hard not to think of *Life Studies* as a series of personal confidences, rather shameful, that one is honor-bound not to reveal."

Of course, as current critics assiduously and correctly stress, in contradistinction to Rosenthal's naive assertion, the "I" of the lyric speaker of poetry is seldom if ever "unequivocally himself," but rather is to some degree a constructed persona. While in some of Lowell's poetry, as I shall later discuss, his persona is ironically detached from the experiences attributed to it, still, in much of it the "I" of the lyrical speaker and his persona are relatively closely aligned.

The confessional mode was a long-overdue dialectical swerving away from the New Critical dogma of the impersonality, of the necessarily detached or inscrutable persona of the lyric speaker. It is impossible to recall how transgressive and antinomian these poems seemed when they first appeared. They treat subject matter that is embarrassing, that "passes the bounds of propriety," and that is above all deemed shameful, putting the reader in the uncomfortable position of being a voyeur who catches glimpses of secrets that ought not to have been revealed. Confessional poetry activates, too, our natural attraction to the outlandish, the outré. The stigma of mental illness in particular—a subject which Lowell broached in his poetry, breaking a powerful taboo—was in the late fifties far stronger than it is now.

As a result of having lived for many years in an ashram in India, I tend to categorize the antinomian strain in poetry in general as tantric in its embrace of that which inspires revulsion as well as attraction; of the forbidden as well as of the sacred; of madness, inspired or otherwise, as well as of the putatively sane; of the daemonic as well as of the divine. In a very real way, the poets of the confessional school, even those whose poems were tamer and more purely domestic than those of Ginsberg, whom I regard as the unsung precursor of the confessional mode, were giving voice, inspired by a tantric or antinomian impulse, to taboo subjects that had previously been kept safely hidden.

In India, the tantric practitioner is playing with fire. If he loses awareness of the real goal of his quest, which is to conquer not only desire but also aversion, revulsion, repugnance, and disgust, he will be in danger of being singed or consumed by that fire. The practitioners of confessional poetry were grounded in no such tradition, were all, in a sense, going it alone, and virtually all of them would be scorched by the fires with which they were playing in deadly earnest.

2.

During my senior year at Harvard, the charismatic doyenne of the confessional school, Anne Sexton, gave a poetry reading in the cavernous spaces of the venerable Sanders Theater, by far the largest venue on campus. The place was packed, and a tingling air of collective anticipation preceded her appearance. When she emerged from the wings, we were in the presence of a strikingly beautiful woman who was, it seemed, more than slightly inebriated. A few uncomfortable moments occurred when Sexton openly flirted—all in good fun—with the young man who was adjusting the height of a standing microphone. After a few tentative readings of her poems, Sexton relaxed, hit her stride, and put on what was more than a merely satisfactory show. It is impossible to imagine any contemporary poet filling such a space or inspiring such an intoxicating buzz of anticipation.

Boston in the mid-seventies, and slightly more narrowly Cambridge, where Lowell was ensconced, was the primary locus of the still-burgeoning confessional school. Plath had earlier studied with Lowell at Boston University, where it was rumored that he had picked up a few tricks of what would become the confessional trade from her, and where Sexton was a teacher. Meanwhile, Frank Bidart, a young acolyte of the school, was beginning his long teaching career at Wellesley and had become a kind of amanuensis to Lowell.

These were the inescapable figures who were very much present at my own creation as a poet. It took considerable energy for me to resist them, and for the complex reasons cited above, to resist Lowell in particular.

Elizabeth Bishop, who was then also teaching at Harvard, travelled in these circles and seemed to be admired by all, but she was by no means a prototypically transgressive, antinomian, confessional poet. Quite to the contrary, her own reticent, reserved poems, though still packing a subliminal emotional wallop, were models not only of decorum but also of a distinctive genius. She was an original, a school of one. Some few of us undergraduate would-be poets at Harvard, myself included, prized her work above Lowell's. Though my spiky, idiosyncratic, fledgling works as a poet were nothing like hers, neither were they, perhaps in part due to her occult influence, anything like Lowell's.

For one brief moment, I was at the epicenter of confessional poetry. While at Harvard, I was a member of *The Harvard Advocate,* its aforementioned redoubtable and long-lived literary rag. During my senior year, my confreres, no doubt with a sense of humor, or more properly with a sense of the absurd, assigned me the task of arranging for and publicizing a series of poetry readings. The last of these was a reading to be given by Lowell. Being deficient in what is now called executive functioning, one of the many relatively new maladies with which children are now routinely diagnosed, and as a result of which they are routinely medicated, I was thoroughly lacking in organizational skills. As a result of my doing my far-from-adequate best, the large lecture hall in which Lowell's reading took place was disappointingly and surprisingly only half full.

My sole remaining task was to introduce Frank Bidart, who was to introduce Lowell. I had never so much as stood in front of a classroom before. Feeling overwhelmed, all semblance of poise deserting me, instead of properly introducing the introducer, who had recently published *Golden State*, his much-lauded first book, I simply blurted "Frank Bidart will be introducing Mr. Lowell" into a microphone that was barely working, then ducked for cover. I immediately imagined, with a paranoid self-centeredness, that I had committed a shameful faux pas.

Immediately after the reading, a party was to take place in the narrow but conveniently nearby confines of Bidart's Cambridge apartment. I was told that as a courtesy to me (obviously unearned), I was invited to attend. Not only were Lowell, Bishop, Sexton, Bidart, Mark Strand, and George Starbuck, the brilliant court jester of the confessional school, in attendance, but so, too, were Octavio Paz, the great Mexican poet who had just won the Nobel prize, and Carlos Fuentes, the much-acclaimed Mexican novelist, both of whom were visiting professors at Harvard in 1975, the year in which the reading took place.

For a full fifteen minutes, I stood cowering and alone in a corner of Bidart's apartment, guzzling gin and tonic from an oversized plastic cup. Eventually, a woman whom I did not recognize sidled away from what seemed to be an engrossing discussion with one of the aforementioned eminences and made her merciful way toward me. I spent much of the next twenty minutes nervously prattling on about Wallace Stevens, parroting insights gleaned from a book on his long poems with the lovely title *On Extended Wings* that I had just finished reading. After having engaged in at least one conversation of some length, I felt I could escape the gathering with some dignity intact. As I was on my way out, someone in a group stationed by the door remarked, "You and Helen seem to have hit it off," whereupon I realized to my chagrin that the gracious woman with whom I had been talking was in fact Helen Vendler, the author of the book whose insights I had just been regurgitating.

Vendler would later become among the most cogent and influential champions of the work of both Lowell and Bishop. Though I respect and admire her criticism, in general I find it slightly too analytical for me, too confident in paraphrasing that which resists paraphrase, too distrustful of the metaphysical and the mystical—though some degree of wariness with respect to both is not only salutary but necessary.

On the other hand, Vendler's writing is blessedly free of the obligatory mash-up of references to fashionable American and European intellectuals that constitute, for most academic writers on poetry, an equally obligatory but often incoherent methodology. Indeed, these no longer merely literary "theorists" should perhaps be rechristened "methodologists," thus indicating that they are at two removes from the poetry that their exegetical endeavors seem intended to supplant. Vendler's writing is a kind of eden or oasis of perspicuity and clarity, while managing to commit the cardinal sin of directly addressing itself to the work at hand.

3.

Lowell, Sexton, Berryman, and the deceased patron saint of the antinomian and the daemonic, Plath, were the "big four" of American confessional poets.

Remarkably, Sexton did not begin writing poetry until the age of twenty-seven. Even more remarkably, her first two books were notable for their extraordinarily deft and entirely self-taught handling of form. This formal rigor seemed to focus and intensify their confessional disclosures. I will cite the briefest, and perhaps the finest of these poems here, an extraordinary, condensed elegy to her parents, who had died within three months of each other.

THE TRUTH THE DEAD KNOW

Gone, I say and walk from church,
refusing the stiff procession to the grave,
letting the dead ride alone in the hearse.

It is June. I am tired of being brave.

We drive to the Cape. I cultivate
myself where the sun gutters from the sky,
where the sea swings in like an iron gate
and we touch. In another county, people die.

My darling, the wind falls in like stones
from the whitehearted water and when we touch
we enter touch entirely. No one's alone.
Men kill for this, or for as much.

And what of the dead? They lie without shoes
in their stone boats. They are more like stone
than the sea would be if it stopped. They refuse
to be blessed, throat, eye and knucklebone.

I can think of few poems of that era whose use of metaphor and simile is as startlingly apposite and moving. Sexton wrote several other poems of almost equal skill and power. The prevailing myth of that era was that poets like Lowell, James Wright, Theodore Roethke, and Berryman "found their voice" by transitioning from formal to free verse. Berryman's work, in fact, remained, albeit in a more relaxed fashion than in his apprentice poems, formal. Sexton, to the contrary, *lost* her voice in the transition from formal to free verse. Eventually, her poems came to seem like a series of slack parodies of Sylvia Plath. This obvious identification with Plath culminated in a horrific way with Sexton's suicide by carbon monoxide poisoning.

Though Plath, Sexton, and Berryman all wrote more than their share of extravagantly confessional poetry, all three, ironically, were at their best when this impulse was to some degree held in check either by the skillful deployment of form or by the occasional celebration of life's radiant possibilities. "The Truth the Dead Know," for example, though rife with images of death, petrification, and loss, also acknowledges the power of married sexual love and entertains the somewhat hopeful notion that "no one's alone." Even though the dead refuse to be blessed, the living can still bless each other.

4.

Although I initially succumbed to the spell of Plath's poems and though, as I have recounted, it was she who was present at my creation as a poet, her imagination only intermittently laid a strong claim on my own. Many of her best-known poems seemed to me punchy but superficial. Poems like "Daddy" and "Lady Lazarus" have a significant impact on first reading, but that impact diminishes rather than increases upon subsequent readings.

Plath, however, produced a small number of what still seem to me extraordinary poems, including a few masterpieces, among them "The Moon and the Yew Tree," "Tulips," and several of her very last poems. The intrepid, determined, and quite long apprenticeship that led to the creation of these poems, and the sheer intensity with which Plath willed herself into being an important poet, are themselves impressive. They also yielded along the way a few odd, distinctive, and strangely powerful poems, including "Electra on Azalea Path" and "Mussel Hunter at Rock Harbor." These poems of Plath's mid-career experimented with dense and often guttural sound effects. Many of them are written in regular stanzaic forms and, perhaps taking a cue from Marianne Moore, are composed not in accentual verse but in syllabics. Syllabic verse assigns a set number of syllables to each line of its repeated stanzas. Unlike Moore's poems, Plath's do not involve eccentric and arresting visual patterning; like them, however, they resist, hedge about, block, and retard, as though abjuring the pleasure principle, the sometimes too-easy fluency of accentual or free verse. Later, Plath's poems grew less dense, more agile, and she developed in her finest, mature work a keen ear for various kinds of free-verse rhythm.

Her mature poems, too, encompass a wide variety of tones, from the savage ironies of her feminist manifesto "The Applicant," to the grotesquely apposite Dr Seuss-like doggerel of "Daddy," in which the poet's father is seen, as through the cowed eyes of a child, as a horrifyingly larger than life and menacing figure; to the brilliant yet grave metaphorical extravagance of "Tulips," which I regard as perhaps her finest poem; to the stately gravity of the aforementioned "The Moon and the Yew Trees"; and finally to the Greek simplicity and economy of many of her last poems, an example of which is "Edge," cited below, in which perfection, whether of the poet's life or of her art, results in a self-destructive sterility. Like many of Plath's last poems, which anticipate her death, it seems written under the aegis of *anake,* of a remorseless, implacable necessity.

EDGE

The woman is perfected.
Her dead

Body wears the smile of accomplishment,
The illusion of a Greek necessity

Flows in the scrolls of her toga,
Her bare

Feet seem to be saying:
We have come so far, it is over.

Each dead child coiled, a white serpent,
One at each little

Pitcher of milk, now empty.
She has folded

Them back into her body as petals
Of a rose close when the garden

Stiffens and odors bleed
From the sweet, deep throats of the night flower.

The moon has nothing to be sad about,
Staring from her hood of bone.

She is used to this sort of thing.
Her blacks crackle and drag.

5.

The last of the "big four" was John Berryman, who quite strenuously objected, with some justice, to being labeled confessional. His *77 Dream Songs*, the work of an extraordinarily erudite and thoughtful poet who now, like Lowell, is too often overlooked, were considered exemplars of the confessional mode but are in fact the effusions of a persona named Henry, who is by no means simply identical to Berryman.

These poems have a jazzy, syncopated, quintessentially American rhythm, a polyglot diction, and a torqued and twisted syntax, which felt startlingly new at the time of their publication. Often riotously funny, the best of them penetrate beneath the merely personal, the realm of the rawly emotional, to a deep, universal, more-than-merely-personal feeling.

Berryman spent twenty years writing properly formal poems, mostly lifeless, hemmed in by New Critical strictures. In other words, he had put in his time before, as a result of some jolt of insight, he broke through to a strange new voice. That breakthrough began to occur in the long, lyric narrative "Homage to Mistress Bradstreet," in which Berryman writes in the voice of the wife of a Protestant divine who was herself a poet. The poem, like the dream songs, is written in a regular but idiosyncratic and rhythmically complex stanzaic form of Berryman's devising.

Although for the most part, the poem is intensely alive, it is almost impermeably dense. Its strongest passage, remarkably, is Bradstreet's recounting of her experience of childbirth. The passage cited below spans the end of the eighteenth to the end of the twenty-first section of Berryman's "Homage" (which is surely an etymologically un-self-consciously ironic title for a poem written in the voice of a woman).

FROM: HOMAGE TO MISTRESS BRADSTREET

...God brandishes. O love, O I love. Kin,
gather. My world is strange
and merciful, ingrown months, blessing a swelling trance.

So squeezed, wince you I scream? I love you & hate
off with you! Ages! *Useless.* Below my waist
he has me in Hell's vise.
Stalling. He let go. Come back: brace
me somewhere. No. No. Yes! Everything down
Hardens I press with horrible joy down
my back cracks like a wrist
Shame I am voiding oh behind it is too late

hide me forever I work thrust I must free
now I all muscles & bones concentrate
what is living from dying?
Simon I must leave you so untidy
Monster you are killing me Be sure
I'll have you later Women do endure
I can *can* no longer
and it passes the wretched trap whelming and I am me

drencht & powerful I did it with my body!
One proud tug greens heaven. Marvelous
unforbidding Majesty.
Swell, imperious bells. I fly.
Mountainous, woman not breaks and will bend:
sways God nearby: anguish comes to an end.
Blossomed Sarah, and I
blossom. Is that thing alive? I hear a famisht howl.

Indebted to Hopkins? *Yes.* Over the top, embarrassing, shameful, transgressive, too intimate, too physically graphic with its talk of voiding behind etc.? *Perhaps.* Yet another boring poem about brittle and lifeless Puritans? *Certainly not.* A confessional poem? *Not yet,* as Berryman couches his poem in the voice of an historically distanced female persona. A transgressive poem? *Certainly.* Berryman's "famisht howl" calls to mind Ginsberg's more famous "Howl."

Is Berryman's appropriation of a female voice a mis-appropriation? Again, I think not, but who am I to judge? Interestingly, all of the finest poems of Randall Jarrell—at one time the most highly regarded critic among the poet/critics I have mentioned—including "Next Day" and "The Woman at the Washington Zoo"— were written in the voices of women, so much so that it led Bishop to remark in a letter to Lowell that she really did not need Jarrell's poems, thank you very much, to provide her with insights about the experience of being a woman. What she thought of Berryman we shall shortly see.

With his dream songs, Berryman found a style and devised a stanzaic form far more accessible than the strangely, hieratically obscure "Homage." The dream songs are composed in a nonce form of Berryman's own devising, consisting of three stanzas of six lines each, with no restriction regarding the length of its lines. The dream songs also entail an intricate rhyme scheme, which, like the songs' line lengths, is also flexible, and which is often subtly varied.

Early in his career, Berryman wrote a series of sonnets to a young woman with whom he had had an extramarital affair, and which, with an eye to keeping his teaching job at Princeton, he for a long time suppressed. Though these sonnets are characterized by the wrenching and distortions of syntax and the sometimes odd and eccentric lexical choices that later appear in the dream songs, they seem to me peculiarly ungainly in rhythm and tortuously inflated in diction and seem to strain awkwardly against the confines of the sonnet.

Several of the best of the dream songs allude directly or indirectly to the suicide of Berryman's father, whose body he discovered, at the age of twelve, shot through the heart, on the beach in front of a bungalow at which the family had been staying. Perhaps the finest of these poems evokes an ineffable, nearly inexpressible sadness that seems to lie at the heart of things.

DREAM SONG 29

There sat down, once, a thing on Henry's heart
só heavy, if he had a hundred years
& more, & weeping, sleepless, in all them time
Henry could not make good.
Starts again always in Henry's ears
The little cough somewhere, an odour, a chime.

And there is another thing he has in mind

like a grave Sienese face a thousand years
would fail to blur the still profiled reproach of. Ghastly,
with open eyes, he attends, blind.
All the bells say: too late. This is not for tears;
thinking.

But never did Henry, as he thought he did,
end anyone and hacks her body up
and hide the pieces, where they may be found.
He knows: he went over everyone, & nobody's missing.
Often he reckons, in the dawn, them up.
Nobody is ever missing.

The last line of this beautiful, grave, haunting poem, "nobody is ever missing," both belies and intensifies the central tragic fact of the poem, which is that someone, someone entirely irreplaceable, is indeed missing, and that no matter how many bodies one reckons or counts up, he will never again be found in the census of the living.

The manner of "Dream Song 29" is relatively dignified. Others of the dream songs present a more-than-merely picaresque protagonist whose adventures are scandalous and unhinged. Often Henry seems to give voice to the mandates of a voracious and ungovernable *id*. The language of primary process often consorts, in the dream songs, with that of an exaggerated literary decorum. The dream sounds are polyphonic, sometimes indulging in a kind of regressive baby talk or, more outrageously, in the language of minstrel shows. Their tone is often sardonic, delighting in a kind of over-the-top gallows humor.

The writing of the dream songs eventually became for Berryman, like Lowell's writing of his sonnets, an obsessive, almost interminable exercise. The similarity in Lowell's and Berryman's relentless exercises in one idiosyncratic form is remarkable.

The first one hundred or so of Berryman's dream songs were dazzling and original productions. I can recall my initial, delightedly mesmerized reaction upon reading *77 Dream Songs,* which had, unlike its nominal confessional confreres, a powerful impact on my own early poetry. But as the sequence "keeps on keeping on" the persona of Henry increasingly becomes identical to Berryman himself, whose poetic gift eventually succumbed to the ravages of alcoholism. Berryman described the writing of his poetry as "performing operations of great delicacy" on himself, painful operations in which he is both surgeon and patient, and which are carried out in full view of those who choose to witness this spectacle. After a valiant effort at recovery from alcoholism, including a touching attempt to rediscover faith in Christ as the ultimate loving intercessor and bestower of forgiveness, Berryman, too, finally resorted to suicide.

Even remarkable poets not fully affiliated with the confessional school—poets like Theodore Roethke, an alcoholic who suffered multiple bouts of psychosis and died in his fifties; and James Wright, likewise alcoholic and seriously depressive; not to mention Delmore Schwartz, the poet who at first seemed to his peers the most promising of their generation, and who suffered a long descent into paranoid psychosis; and finally Bishop, yet another alcoholic who endured profound travails of her own—seemed nevertheless implicated in a pervasive generational malaise.

After suffering a series of depressions, Randall Jarrell, author of the posthumously published *The Lost World* ("Back in Los Angeles, we / missed Los Angeles"), walking on foot on the siding of an interstate highway seemed, according to the testimony of an eyewitness, to swerve into the path of an oncoming truck. His death, too, was deemed a likely suicide. Early on, he had been a vital critical champion of Lowell. Jarrell had written, famously, in an essay on Wallace Stevens that "a good poet is a someone who manages, in a lifetime of standing out in thunderstorms, to be struck by lightening five or six times." Later in his life, it likely seemed to him that when he compared himself to some of his poetic peers, lightning had not struck him often enough. The author of *Poetry and the Age,* still a model of passionately argued criticism, as willing to damn and make enemies as to praise and cultivate friends, upon whose words a generation of poets had hung, had for too long been sidelined, his spirit broken, teaching English composition in an obscure teacher's college in North Carolina.

The only generation of English poets even remotely as ill-starred came of age in the mid-eighteenth century, after Pope and his fellow Augustans, and before the rise of the Romantics. Smart, Collins, and Cowper all experienced bouts of psychosis and religious mania. Thomas Gray, the most renowned poet of this generation, the author, famously, of "Elegy Written in a Country Churchyard," an avowed atheist, published only thirteen poems during his lifetime and suffered an unrelenting anhedonia, constantly musing on the pointlessness of life in the face of certain annihilation. The generation that included the confessional poets was also interstitial, coming of age after the last of the high Modernists and before the notably various, markedly hardier generation including Ashbery, Ammons, Merrill, and Merwin that followed them.

6.

Alone among the confessional "big four," Lowell, who seemed, despite his mental afflictions, to have had a constitution strong enough to endure them as well as a kind of fundamental and courageous allegiance to life, never seemed to have been seriously tempted to commit suicide. It would be a regrettable omission not to include a poem by Lowell as the culmination of this brief tour of the poets who were in the ascendance during my youth. The ensuing discussion of Lowell's poem, "Man and Wife," from *Life Studies* will serve, I hope, to bridge the gap between my early condemnation of Lowell that is the subject of the previous chapter and the more mature appreciation of his work that is the subject of the succeeding one. I cite the poem in full below.

MAN AND WIFE

Tamed by *Miltown*, we lie on Mother's bed;
the rising sun in war paint dyes us red;
in broad daylight her gilded bed-posts shine,
abandoned, almost Dionysian.
At last the trees are green on Marlborough Street,
blossoms on our magnolia ignite
the morning with their murderous five day's white.
All night I've held your hand,
as if you had
a fourth time faced the kingdom of the mad—
its hackneyed speech, its homicidal eye—
and dragged me home alive. . . . Oh my *Petite,*
clearest of all God's creatures, still all air and nerve:
you were in your twenties, and I,
once hand on glass
and heart in mouth,
outdrank the Rahvs in the heat
of Greenwich Village, fainting at your feet—
too boiled and shy
and poker-faced to make a pass,
while the shrill verve
of your invective scorched the traditional South.

Now twelve years later, you turn your back.
Sleepless, you hold
your pillow to your hollows like a child;
your old-fashioned tirade—
loving, rapid, merciless—
breaks like the Atlantic Ocean on my head.

In the previous chapter, my discussion of *Life Studies* centered on poems that I found, and to some degree still find, either claustrophobically self-regarding or cold-bloodedly cruel. "Man and Wife" is clearly a poem of a different kind. It is in no way, of course, a cruel poem. Quite to the contrary, it is an enormously affecting love poem to his wife, the brilliant novelist, short-story writer, and critic, Elizabeth Hardwick, chief among the many brilliant women to whom Lowell was attracted, who was pointedly not herself a New England WASP, but who hailed from "the traditional South," a region of the county in which Lowell had found something like a safe harbor as a young man.

"Man and Wife," for all of its evocation of affection, has, initially at least, a somewhat distanced quality, as though Lowell is viewing his persona in the poem from outside its frame, an effect introduced by the generic title of the poem. This kind of distancing or doubling of the self affords Lowell the opportunity to view himself as protagonist with some measure of irony and humor, both of which are reflective of a kind of objective, sane version of a too often destabilized self.

"Man and Wife," with its sinuously uncoiling, irregularly rhymed lines that expand or contract at the will—or rather at the prompting of a highly developed instinct—of the poet, and with its iambic base that allows for multiple line lengths as the poem unfolds, seems to me a perfectly sustained and dynamic sonic gesture that is reminiscent of the opening section of "The Quaker Graveyard at Nantucket."

The poem's first four lines, a kind of quatrain in heroic couplets, could only have been written by Lowell:

> Tamed by *Miltown*, we lie on Mother's bed;
> the rising sun in war paint dyes us red;
> in broad daylight her gilded bed-posts shine,
> abandoned, almost Dionysian.

Miltown was a barbiturate sedative, an anti-anxiolytic and sleeping aid that was a drug of choice in the fifties. Lowell and Hardwick are glimpsed lying languidly in his mother's bed, which introduces a humorous hint of the incestuous. They are dyed in an incongruously vivid red war paint by the sun, in a state anything but militant or aroused, between gilded, ironically phallic, Dionysian bedposts. Outside, it is spring, the season of eros, but the magnolias that line what Lowell elsewhere describes as "hardy passionate Marlborough Street" are described as flammable and murderous, as though life itself is a threat to the barely living.

The line "All night I've held your hand" touchingly follows, as does a tribute to Hardwick, who stood with and by Lowell as he endured, multiple times, and not only in dreams, "the kingdom of the mad," its "homicidal eye" semantically rhyming with the "murderous five day's white" of the magnolias.

After the ellipsis in line twelve, the poet addresses his wife with a term of endearment, "Oh my *Petite* / clearest of all God's creatures, still all air and nerve." The word "still" launches the poet into a recollection of his earliest encounter with Hardwick, at whose feet, overwhelmed, he hyperbolically recalls himself having fainted while at the same time listening to "the shrill verve" of her "invective." The

Rahvs referred to in the poem are Phillip Rahv, the editor of the left-leaning *Partisan Review*, and his wife, around whom a cenacle of like-minded, left-wing poets and novelists gravitated. Hardwick, who was possessed of considerable wit, was an occasional polemicist, and here her invective scorches, like Sherman's march, a traditional South that still brutalized its black citizens.

The poems final stanza returns to the present:

> Now twelve years later, you turn your back.
> Sleepless, you hold
> your pillow to your hollows like a child;

Hardwick's clutching of the pillow like a child presents her in a more vulnerable state and recalls her earlier almost maternal holding of Lowell's hand. Yet,

> your old-fashioned tirade—
> loving, rapid, merciless—
> breaks like the Atlantic Ocean on my head.

This "tirade," reminiscent of the "invective" in the previous stanza, is likened to an elemental force and yet is fundamentally also experienced as "loving."

"Man and Wife" is not only an immensely skillful poem but a remarkably vivid portrait of a marriage that has lasted through more than its share of upheavals. Ultimately the poem is a celebration of the eros that seemed to so threaten its protagonist at its outset. The poem enacts the emergence from the impotence of depression to the vitality of a renewed life force. The uneasy lassitude of the poem's opening has been overcome. Finally, a man's relationship with his wife, unlike that with his parents or relatives, particularly when they are seen as pitiful or impotent, is ideally generative, productive, like spring, of new life.

There is nothing of Lowell's off-putting grandiosity in this poem. In "Man and Wife," Lowell himself, in contradistinction to his poems about his parents and the manic, religious, Puritan revenge fantasies that so repelled me as a young man, appears in a more sympathetic light.

It is to my more mature, more flattering reappraisal of Lowell's work that I shall now turn.

~ CHAPTER 6 ~

COMING TO TERMS WITH LOWELL

1.

I, too, like Lowell, as previously mentioned, have suffered throughout my life multiple debilitating episodes of depression, resulting in humiliating and dehumanizing hospitalizations, three of which occurred before my mid-thirties, by which point I increasingly felt admiration for Lowell's resilience, which I came to regard as a form of admirable courage. Accordingly, at first warily, I allowed myself to be as much as possible a same-hearted reader of Lowell, laying myself open to a very different experience of his work.

Lowell suffered an affliction that I, thankfully, did not and do not share. His frequent bouts of mania were so intense that they led to periods of psychosis. When he was in a full-blown episode, it took the combined force of many men to subdue the greatly amplified physical strength of an already physically strong man, an amplification that was itself a symptom of manic psychosis, and to send him packing off to the cruel if relatively benign confines of the locked mental ward at McLean Hospital.

Apart from such alarming incidents, Lowell's mania led him to perform any number of acts, from writing screeds in praise of Hitler; to engaging in physical violence like his abuse of Jean Stafford; to indulging, while married to his second wife, Elizabeth Hardwick, in numerous, often sexually consummated infatuations with younger women, which he subsequently abhorred, and which retrospectively subjected him to agonizing guilt and remorse. This kind of experience of shame, surely among the most toxic of feelings, is entirely typical of those whose experiences of mania cause them to act out in ways that they subsequently deplore, and that offend their moral sense, subjecting them to a lacerating self-condemnation, which intensifies the periods of depression that inevitably follow mania. And yet in our era of increasing tolerance for the marginalized and the afflicted, we are still perhaps too willing to judge Lowell who, although benefiting from privilege, was scourged by a disease that was anything but a privilege.

Ironically, while condemning Lowell for assuming the role of prophet and judge, I set myself up, as a young man, as a remorseless judge not only of Lowell's poems but of his character as well. The time eventually came for me to lay aside my juridical robes. Also ironically, even as Lowell's reputation since his death has been plummeting, my own estimation of his work has been rising, has become far more generous. It includes the recognition that Lowell, despite his afflictions, continued to grow as a human being even in periods in which he was stuck as a poet. He did not, like the spider in his poem on Jonathan Edwards, and like others of the benighted confessional school, simply stretch out his feet, metrical or otherwise, and die. Instead, in both his life and his work, he kept reentering the fray. His hunger for life, for human connection, was never abandoned and in fact seemed to grow over time. This growth is most evident in his remarkable final book, *Day by Day*, a late, touchingly elegiac celebration of eros in all of its forms as well as a mournful and bitter acceptance of both psychic pain and the depredations of old age and physical illness. It is to my more mature re-evaluation of Lowell's work that I will now turn.

2.

To begin again, briefly, at the beginning: in *Lord Weary's Castle*, though the majority of its poems now feel dated, Lowell did manage to create, in poems including "The Quaker Graveyard in Nantucket," "Mr Edwards and the Spider," and even "Colloquy at Black Rock," something—in the words of "Epilogue," the exquisite last poem of his last book, *Day by Day*—"imagined not recalled," poems of a visionary intensity, which is conveyed not by their sense or absence of sense but by a considerable rhetorical and rhythmical power that managed to sweep all aside in its wake—including the New Critical demand for intellectual complexity and coherence. Certainly "Quaker Graveyard," a kind of juggernaut, bowled me over when I first read it. It still retains its sheer linguistic impact. The fact that I did not and largely still do not—in part because of my own Neo-Romantic, metaphysical predilections, in part because of the vagaries of my own temperament—find Lowell's Neo-Puritan, Neo-Catholic, Neo-Classical vision congenial or sympathetic, or that I find in its dark sublimity, in its extremity, more than a hint of the pathological, is largely beside the point. I am told and am willing to concede that one does not have to subscribe to Pound's politics to admire *The Cantos,* whose most moving sequence, the "Pisan Cantos," is the work of a madman—in Pound's case, one in the grip of paranoid schizophrenia.

In my prior treatment of *Life Studies*, I focused chiefly on those poems that involved Lowell's indictments of his family. But a number of the poems in *Life Studies*, including the previously discussed "Man and Wife," fall into several other categories: those that deal with marriage and fatherhood; those that are touching tributes to friends, many of them poets; those that are preoccupied with literary figures from the past who were so present to Lowell that they might as well have been friends; and perhaps most significantly, those that directly confront the poet's own experience.

These poems tend to be bemused, humorous, delighting in their subjects' eccentricities and human foibles while at the same time the poet implicitly recognizes his own. Above all, like "Man and Wife," they are affectionate. Lowell's tone in these poems, often gently ironic, is entirely different from that of the hanging judge of *Lord Weary's Castle* or of the contemptuous son who elsewhere in *Life Studies* is unable to forgive his parents.

Among the most touching of the poems in *Life Studies* is "To Delmore Schwartz." Schwartz's debut collection of stories and poems, *In Dreams Begin Responsibilities*, led to his being regarded by those of his peers nurtured by the New Criticism as the most talented and promising poet among them. His erudition, wit, and brilliance, and his extraordinary improvised intellectual riffs as a talker, were legendary. But by his early forties, something had begun to go seriously off the rails. Schwartz had labored for years over a long epic poem in verse, "Genesis," and later over a drama in blank verse, neither of which, when finally published, were critically well-received.

It gradually became clear that Schwartz's promise as a poet would not be fulfilled. He continued to write, producing the sprawling, unkempt, rhythmically slack poems that, along with his finally finished verse drama, would later appear in his book *Summer Knowledge*. To those who had known Schwartz as a young man, the book must have been painful to read. Eventually, Schwartz became increasingly reclusive and receded from view. Gradually, toward the end of his life, he, like Pound, descended into paranoid psychosis. In his last five or six years, he lived in complete isolation, refusing to see or talk with friends, in a room in Manhattan's fabled Chelsea Hotel, the last stop for a number of troubled writers. After he died of a heart attack in 1966 at the age of fifty-two, it took the police several days to discover and identify his already decomposing body.

Lowell's poem, as a head-note makes clear, is set in 1946, when Schwartz and Lowell briefly lived together in Cambridge. The poem begins with a long anecdote about a duck that Schwartz had killed and had then, rather ineptly, preserved. The duck

> . . .was your first kill: you had rushed it home,
> pickled in a tin wastebasket of rum—
> It looked through us, as if it'd died dead drunk.

The duck becomes something of an odd tutelary deity or presiding genius in the household they shared:

> . . . And there,
> perched on my trunk and typing-table,
> it cooled our universal
> *Angst* a moment, Delmore. We drank and eyed
> the chicken-hearted shadows of the world.
> Underseas fellows, nobly mad,
> we talked away our friends. "Let Joyce and Freud,
> the Masters of Joy,
> be our guests here," you said. The room was filled
> with cigarette smoke circling the paranoid,
> inert gaze of Coleridge, back
> from Malta — his eyes lost in flesh, lips baked and black.
> your tiger kitten, Oranges,
> cartwheeled for joy in a ball of snarls.
> You said:
> *"We poets in our youth begin in sadness;*
> *thereof in the end come despondency and madness;*
> Stalin has had two cerebral hemorrhages."
> The Charles
> River was turning silver. In the ebb-
> light of morning, we stuck
> the duck
> -s' web-
> foot, like a candle, in a quart of gin we'd killed.

Initially, the poem seems a witty, delightfully anecdotal, "boys will be boys" account of the friendship between two high-spirited young males who have pulled an all-nighter together, excitedly bantering. These boys, however, judging by the date on the poem's head note, were in fact, somewhat disconcertingly, in Lowell's case twenty-nine, and in Schwartz's several years older. The two poets humorously, romantically, regard themselves as sub-aquatic "underseas fellows, nobly mad," sufferers from the kind of universal angst young poets often used to cultivate. They are an alliance of two, conscious of their exceptional brilliance, a perch from which they regard, with mutual disdain, the "chicken-hearted shadows" of a world unredeemed by poetry. Their talk is playful, is analogous to and as innocent as the play of Schwartz's kitten, Oranges, who as they talked "cartwheeled for joy in a ball of snarls." At the same time, Schwartz invites two "Masters of Joy," Joyce and Freud, to be guests in the room that he and Lowell share. The reference to Freud is at once genuinely admiring and ironic: he is ordinarily thought of as a proponent of the reality principle rather than as a master of unbridled joy.

Later, it becomes clear that another presiding tutelary deity, a picture of Coleridge, has joined the embalmed duck. His "inert gaze" echoes the blind, lifeless gaze of the duck whose eyes, as is disclosed earlier in the poem, have been gruesomely nailed open by Schwartz in his first clumsy foray as a taxidermist. The poem that begins with a humorous depiction of a duck that, having been "pickled in rum, looked through us, as if it'd died dead drunk," ends with its two poet/protagonists having "killed a quart of gin" during their all-night conversation. They are pickled, though not yet embalmed, by alcohol. Ultimately the poem's two tutelary deities, impotent, blind, and lifeless, seem not so much beneficent presiding divinities as daemonic totems.

Schwartz intones a clumsy, slight misquotation of the famous lines from Wordsworth: "We Poets in our youth begin in gladness; / But thereof comes in the end despondency and madness," lines that proved, sadly, to be prophetic of Wordsworth's fate. After his rift with Coleridge, Wordsworth wrote increasingly desiccated poems drained of his former imaginative energy. The reference to Coleridge's "paranoid gaze" cannot help but call to mind Schwartz's subsequent descent into paranoid schizophrenia. Wordsworth's lines are prophetic, of course, not only of Schwartz's fate, but also of the travails suffered by Lowell and by a number poets of his generation.

The wit and humor in the poem are ultimately overwhelmed by a kind of retrospective sadness. When Coleridge is invoked, it is not my chosen Coleridge, who wrote paeans to the imagination, but another equally characteristic Coleridge whose terrible enslavement to the opiate laudanum lurched fully and finally out of control during a lonely sojourn at Malta that was intended to have an opposite, curative effect. When he returned home, his appearance shocked his friends. His distinctive features had been obliterated, and he seemed a ruin of himself. As we have seen, an inordinate number of the poets of Lowell's generation likewise struggled with addiction, though their drug of choice was alcohol.

Lowell's poem ends with a kind of false dawn whose light is curiously depicted as "ebbing." The ineptly preserved duck, one of the poem's daemonic presiding deities, is dethroned from his perch, his webbed foot unceremoniously stuck in the neck of a newly opened and newly emptied, or "killed," bottle of gin.

In its use of memory, "To Delmore Schwartz" involves a kind of Wordsworth-like doubling of the self, capturing a brief moment in time while from a later perspective suggesting not, as in Wordsworth's "Tintern Abbey," the present's revitalizing link with the past, but rather time's ongoing ravages. But above all, it is a loving tribute to Schwartz who, though not yet dead at the time of the poem's writing, was already among the lost and the disappeared.

Lowell's poems on friends and literary peers in *Life Studies* are the precursors of many more such poems in volumes to come. But perhaps the most startling of the poems in *Life Studies* are those on Lowell's experience of himself, in some of which he regards himself with the same bemused, ironic, detached, sometimes humorous, mostly sympathetic eye that he trains upon his friends.

Among these poems is "Memories of West Street and Lepke," which recalls Lowell's year-long incarceration for conscientious objection to World War Two, and which contains the memorable lines, "I was a fire-breathing Catholic C.O., / and made my manic statement, / telling off the state and president." Lowell is making rueful, sardonic sport here of the deluded and self-important young man, infatuated with his status as a Lowell, who had sent the grossly inappropriate, too-intimate letter to President Roosevelt to which I have previously referred.

The poem winds down with a reference to the pathetically reduced figure of "*Murder Incorporated's* Czar Lepke," his fellow inmate.

> Flabby, bald, lobotomized,
> he drifted in a sheepish calm,
> where no agonizing reappraisal
> jarred his concentration on the electric chair
> hanging like an oasis in his air
> of lost connections. . .

Lowell's period of incarceration is depicted, like Lepke's, as a kind of surreal oasis in which he merely drifts, barely in touch with the outside world, through an "air of lost connections." From the retrospective vantage point of the poem, Lowell, himself a reduced figure, has also lost connection to the prophetic certainties that had once caused his incarceration.

Here as elsewhere in *Life Studies,* Lowell struggles with the loss of a religious, morally sanctioned voice; grapples with, in the words of Robert Frost, "what to do with a diminished thing." Lowell's "seed time," from the perspective of "Memories of West Street and Lepke" and of *Life Studies* as a whole, can be seen as mere regrettable delusion, which necessitates an ironic distancing, a self-doubt that is wholly absent in his earlier work. During what he refers to in "Memories of West Street and Lepke" as the "tranquilized," if not quite the lobotomized, fifties, Lowell for a long time seemed to himself to have lost his way as a poet, a state which necessitated the "agonizing reappraisal" that eventually resulted in the writing of *Life Studies.* As opposed to the strong closure that characterized his poems of the now bygone epoch of *Lord Weary's Castle,* "Memories of West Street and Lepke" concludes with a nonterminal ellipsis, with a kind of dangling open-endedness.

Among the best known of Lowell's poems on his own experience is "Waking in the Blue," written about another kind of incarceration, one of Lowell's many hospitalizations in a locked ward at McLean's Hospital, the preferred place for Boston Brahmins to warehouse their inbred, unmanageably mad family members, whether briefly or for years.

In profound depression, as in manic psychosis, all sense of free agency is lost, a felt lack that was exacerbated in the case of Lowell by his frequent incarcerations in the locked wards of mental hospitals. It is impossible for those who have not been afflicted with similar states and who have not spent long sojourns imprisoned in hospitals to understand how existentially terrifying, how traumatic, even one such experience can be. Reduced by the travails of depression to a gutted, unrecognizable shell of oneself, one merely waits, anxiously hopes, day after day whose blank duration seems endless, for the inexpressible darkness to lift.

Seen in the context of a such an incarceration, "Waking in the Blue" is particularly remarkable for its ironic detachment. Lowell trains a humorous eye not only on himself but on his tribe of fellow "Mayflower screwballs." Again, Lowell's tone here is remarkably different from that of *Lord Weary's Castle*, which is almost completely self-serious and without irony. I cite several stanzas from the poem below.

> The night attendant, a B.U. sophomore,
> rouses from the mare's-nest of his drowsy head
> propped on *The Meaning of Meaning*.
> He catwalks down our corridor.
>
> ....
>
> What use is my sense of humor?
> I grin at Stanley, now sunk in his sixties,
> once a Harvard all-American fullback,
> (if such were possible!)
> still hoarding the build of a boy in his twenties,
> as he soaks, a ramrod
> with the muscle of a seal
> in his long tub,
> vaguely urinous from the Victorian plumbing.
> A kingly granite profile in a crimson gold-cap,
> worn all day, all night,
> he thinks only of his figure,
> of slimming on sherbet and ginger ale —
> more cut off from words than a seal.
>
> ...
>
> In between the limits of day,
> hours and hours go by under the crew haircuts
> and slightly too little nonsensical bachelor twinkle
> of the Roman Catholic attendants.
> (There are no Mayflower
> screwballs in the Catholic Church.)

After a hearty New England breakfast,
I weigh two hundred pounds
this morning. Cock of the walk,
I strut in my turtle-necked French sailor's jersey
before the metal shaving mirrors,
and see the shaky future grow familiar
in the pinched, indigenous faces.
of these thoroughbred mental cases,
twice my age and half my weight.
We are all old-timers,
each of us holds a locked razor.

Though Lowell's ironic distancing of his authorial from his remembered self and its experiences is in some way admirable, the tone of the poem is perhaps slightly too close to ridicule, to the cool contempt to which Lowell subjects his father elsewhere in the volume. Nevertheless, and again, how different is Lowell's treatment of himself in this poem from the sententious, parochial, unearned regard for himself as a Lowell that he was once far more prone to indulge.

As previously mentioned, Lowell's poems on his own experience initially seemed to me narcissistically, unbecomingly self-obsessed. I knew as a young man that Lowell suffered from repeated bouts of depression. I did not know the depth and frequency of Lowell's experiences of madness. In Lowell's era, the Freudian notion that one could overcome all forms of mental illness by cleaving to the reality principle and coming to know oneself and one's unconscious motivations was at the height of its prestige. Seen from this perspective, Lowell's poems on himself seem like desperate, poignant attempts to understand himself, to comprehend an illness which is by its very nature, we now know, incomprehensible.

In "Skunk Hour," *Life Studies'* crowning achievement and one of Lowell's undoubted masterpieces, he abandons the ironic tone of poems like "Waking in the Blue." Nakedly and with a peculiar intensity of feeling, yet with great art and formal control, he confronts, in six irregularly rhymed six-line stanzas, a dark night of the soul engendered by depression. Unlike many of Lowell's arbitrarily enjambed exercises in free verse, and like "Man and Wife," the first stanza of "The Quaker Graveyard in Nantucket," and several of his other felicitous hybrids of free and formal verse, "Skunk Hour" unfolds as a perfectly calibrated sonic gesture.

In "Skunk Hour," Lowell's profound malaise is translated into something more than merely personal; he brilliantly reflects and indicts the malaise of a loveless and lifelessly desiccated New England culture now in decline. In "Skunk Hour," a mind "not right" prophetically anatomizes and condemns a time and a place—in this case Castine, a small coastal town in Maine to which Lowell often returned—that are now out of joint. Lowell proclaims in "Skunk Hour" that "the season's ill." The season in question is fall, a literal fall that is also a figurative one.

"Skunk Hour" suggests that a once secure, vertical, upstanding, yet too rigid and hierarchical social structure has now, like a mutating strand of DNA, become deleteriously scrambled. The poem begins with "Nautilus Island's hermit / heiress" who lives "above the sea," who was once doubtless at the top of the town's social hierarchy but is now senile, "in her dotage." She, like the town over which she presides, is now in decline. Meanwhile, her once humble tenant farmer, somewhat ludicrously, now holds the exalted position of the town's "first selectman," an archaic-sounding, typically New England term that is equivalent to "mayor." The town's "summer millionaire" having apparently died or fallen from financial grace, has sold his "nine-knot yawl" to lobstermen.

The town's "chalk-dry and spar spire / of the Trinitarian Church" is, as in so many New England towns, its most prominent and visible structure and establishes a vertical, spiritual dimension, reaching heavenward while remaining rooted to earth. Somewhat strangely, however, Lowell describes the spire as "spar," a noun used as an adjective, which is not only a subliminal pun for "spare" but also a nautical term for a wooden beam, set at an oblique angle to the masts of old schooners, which held the largest of their sails in place. Thus the church's spire, reminiscent of the "weathervane cod" that "sticks like a fishbone / in the city's throat" in "For the Union Dead," is an implicit indictment of a fallen culture; at the same time, in this poem, it is metaphorically not upright like a mast but tilted like a yardarm, however slightly, toward a fallen earth whose beautiful fall foliage is described as a "red fox stain," blighted by something akin to original sin; and toward a now lifeless past whose spiritual values belong to a bygone era.

Multiple references to money and the capricious power conferred by it, which have usurped those values as the chief currency in the town, are implicit or explicit in "Skunk Hour." The town's hermit heiress is wealthy enough to buy up "all the eyesores facing her shore." The town's bankrupt summer millionaire has fallen from grace and departed. Its "fairy decorator," who occupies an equivocal place in the town's social hierarchy, finds "no money in his work, / he'd rather marry."

The town's citizens, rather than participating in a vibrant community, live in a terrible, loveless, sterile isolation that seems to proffer no viable future. Its "hermit heiress," "Thirsting for / the hierarchic privacy / of Queen Victoria's century," faces backward in time, and even before descending into the isolation of senility has expunged all traces of human others from her view. The shop of the town's "fairy decorator" enshrines its merely decorative, artificial "fishnet" and "cobbler's bench and awl"—painted a somewhat ludicrous orange to reflect the season—which are lifeless, vestigial effigies of mostly bygone or declining trades, while the decorator himself is also trapped in an unhappy isolation. The marriage he longs for, however, is not envisaged as an affair of the heart but as a mere monetary transaction. One imagines that it, too, even if in some unlikely event it were to prove possible, would be loveless, lifeless, and childless, oriented toward no generative future.

Finally, at the beginning of the poem's fifth stanza, the medial point of the poem in which day switches to night, we are introduced to the poet himself, who is likewise trapped in the terrible isolation of mental illness, and who is reduced to watching the "hulls" (a metaphor picking up on the poem's prior nautical imagery) of cars in a local lover's lane while his own car's radio bleats "Love, O careless Love . . . " In this poem of multiple correspondences, even the word "bleats" harkens back to the incongruous pastoral image of the heiress' "farmer" shepherding her sheep high above the sea. The farmer's task, too, is inessential, merely decorative, and is as well a kind of parody of the typical Christian pastoral imagery of Christ shepherding his flock.

Lowell sees his illness as analogous to a fallen state. Certainly the sexual voyeurism of the poem's protagonist suggests if not a fallen, at least a degraded condition. I have mentioned the voyeuristic tendency endemic to confessional poetry. We are placed, in reading "Skunk Hour," in the uncomfortable position of being voyeurs of a voyeur. The poet/speaker, who is clearly closely aligned with Lowell, proclaims with the typical grandiosity that is the flip side of depression, "I myself am hell," echoing Satan's statement, "Which way I fly is Hell; myself am Hell" from Milton's *Paradise Lost*. Since we as readers are more than usually identified with Lowell, the poem and the pathetic scene that it unfolds comes close to conveying what the hell of depression with its "ill-spirit sob in each blood cell" must have felt like to him.

At the same time, as Lowell has suggested, the poem's speaker's illness reflects St. John of the Cross' purgatorial dark night of the soul. Its reference to his car climbing "the hill's skull" is to Golgotha, the hill outside of Jerusalem on which Christ was crucified. It is thus, though elevated, antithetical to the height of "Nautilus Island's hermit / heiress," the perch above the sea with which the poem begins. Thus the poem itself, as I shall soon explore, holds open the possibility of redemption, or at least of renewal.

After proclaiming that "I myself am hell," the poet/speaker proclaims, highlighting his sense of isolation, that "nobody's here," nobody that is, except for skunks that

> ... march on their soles up Main Street:
> white stripes, moonstruck eyes' red fire
> under the chalk-dry and spar spire
> of the Trinitarian Church.

In an ultimate inversion of the hierarchical, the skunks usurp the main street of the town as though they are triumphant congregants marching down the aisle of the

Congregationalist Church. Their white stripes mime the color of the church, while their moonstruck eyes' red fire, a somewhat menacing image, also chromatically echoes, of course, the "red fox stain covering Blue Hill," the orange of the fairy decorator's fishnet and cobbler's bench, and the encompassing, overall color of fall, of Lowell's ill season.

And yet the skunks are familial and communal, unlike the isolated citizens of a village that they, too, inhabit. Though they are mere scavengers, the least among God's creatures, they are vividly and fiercely alive. "Skunk Hour" concludes with a sighting by Lowell of a mother skunk and her progeny in his back yard. Breathing in a suddenly "rich air," Lowell observes:

> a mother skunk with her column of kittens swills the garbage pail.
> She jabs her wedge-head in a cup
> of sour cream, drops her ostrich tail,
> and will not scare.

Unlike poor, neurotic man, the mother skunk serenely drops her tail and does not scare. She is an unlikely emissary of a reviving eros, of a staunch life source, and of a will to survive. Though she knows nothing of sin or redemption, she anticipates the possibility of a renewed life for the poem's speaker and, of course, for Lowell himself.

"Skunk Hour" is remarkable for its skeins of interrelated images that are at the same time related to other such skeins of metaphors and images, for coherent sets of correspondences that belie and counterbalance the alienated state of both the poem's speaker and of the venal, fragmented society that he indicts.

Finally, "Skunk Hour," which, though personal, outstrips the merely personal, reclaims again something like a prophetic voice, leading Lowell, if only temporarily, out of the wilderness of enervation and self-doubt in which he felt immured after the heady, manic high that produced *Lord Weary's Castle* had passed.

In subsequent poems, Lowell continues to confront head-on his experiences of mental illness and the troubling actions and consequences they sometimes entailed. *For the Union Dead*, a kind of companion piece to *Life Studies*, contains several such poems, including "Eye and Tooth," which concludes with the line "I am tired. / Everyone's tired of my turmoil."

The book is also notable for the poem from which it derives its title, which is among Lowell's finest. Alas, to do "For the Union Dead" any kind of justice would require an essay of considerable length. I will do Lowell the disservice of almost passing over this poem here, with the exception of making a few observations, the first being that "For the Union Dead" unites, like "Skunk Hour," the virtues of Lowell's formal poems with those in free verse. "For the Union Dead," with its repeated four-line stanzas in lines of varying lengths and its irregularly regular end rhymes, has much in common formally with "Skunk Hour." The old apocalyptic concerns of Lowell's poetry reappear, more convincingly than in Lowell's *Lord Weary's Castle*, in reference to the threat of possible nuclear annihilation, a horrific version of the sublime that was very much on the minds of most people during the early sixties, less than two decades after Hiroshima, when the poem was written.

The poem, again like "Skunk Hour," is notable for its radical, pervasive use of metaphor, with multiple, rich strands of metaphor themselves metaphorically related to other such strands, all contributing to a dense, textured, endlessly internally refracted or reflected sense of how Boston lives not only on the page but also presumably in the poet's mind and heart, in the unplumbable depths signified by its opening reference to a childhood memory of the now-defunct South Boston aquarium. "I often sigh still," Lowell writes, "for the dark downward and vegetating kingdom / of the fish and reptile"—a line that is surely among Lowell's most characteristic, both with respect to the aquatic or amphibious subjects that recur frequently in his poetry, and with respect to the sound of the line, its wonderful decrescendo, its prolonged, elegiac, falling cadence. The poem is not only a powerfully conflicted evocation and indictment of Boston in the early sixties but an atavistic evocation of childhood itself, which, though to an unusual degree still alive in Lowell, is also unfathomable in its hidden, impossible-to-sound depths. Near the end of the poem, the adult poet sits rapt before the TV as he once, as a child, had sat rapt before the glass of the old aquarium. He beholds on its screen the "drained faces of Negro school-children rise like balloons," rising as bubbles once rose just out of touch behind the glass in the waters of the now-lost aquarium.

And yet like "Skunk Hour," though grounded in the personal, "For the Union Dead" transcends the merely personal. It is a self-consciously public poem in which Lowell reclaims, more vigorously than in "Skunk Hour," and far more subtly than in *Lord Weary's Castle*, something of a prophetic voice whose masterfully assured cadences triumphantly transcend the self-doubting enervation that is characteristic of, and in some cases the theme of, some of the poems of *Life Studies* and *For The Union Dead*.

Near the Ocean, the book that succeeds *For the Union Dead*, is among Lowell's finest. It includes, most notably, "Waking Early Sunday Morning," the first in a suite of poems that are a happy reversion, Lowell's last, to strictly formal verse.

"Waking Early Sunday Morning," another self-consciously public poem whose subject is the Vietnam War presided over by "the President / girdled by his establishment," is at the same time a paean to the influx of sexual vitality the poet feels upon emerging from a depression. In his less than full-blown manic phases, phases of renewed energy, Lowell's resurgent interest in his poetic enterprise, and in matters sexual and political, were enthusiasms or excitements that overlapped, as though they were different aspects of the same power, a power that, especially in his political poems, is a subject that itself endlessly fascinates Lowell. The same combustible elements were also tragically prominent, more disturbingly and unproductively, in Lowell's full-blown episodes of mania.

"Waking Early Sunday Morning" has, like "The Quaker Graveyard at Nantucket," the almost visionary, dynamic, propulsive force of something "imagined, not recalled." It is exquisitely written in eight-line, four-beat stanzas with rhyming and off-rhyming couplets. It is clearly modeled after and reminiscent of Andrew Marvell, the most elegant, sophisticated, urbane, and uncanny of seventeenth-century English metaphysical poets. The language of "Waking Early Sunday Morning," which combines abstraction with a subtle but intense sensuousness, a too-often overlooked attribute of Lowell's poetry, is answerable to Stevens' dictum in *Notes Toward a Supreme Fiction*: "It Must Give Pleasure." I cite, almost at random, one of its stanzas here.

> I watch a glass of water wet
> with a fine fuzz of icy sweat,
> silvery colors touched with sky,
> serene in their neutrality—
> yet if I shift, or change my mood,
> I see some object made of wood,
> background behind it of brown grain,
> to darken it, but not to stain.

As both "Waking Early Sunday Morning" and the suite of poems that comprise *Near the Ocean* progress, however, the sensuous immediacy and power with which they commence become increasingly inflected by dark intimations of the ebbing of that power, of a depression that by this time Lowell surely knew was inevitably to follow.

3.

Lowell's multiple translations, imitations, adaptations, responses to, and sometimes appropriations of the work of others, which I passed over in my first, youthful reading of Lowell's work, merit mentioning here. Written concurrently with *For The Union Dead* and *Near The Ocean*, in the years immediately prior to the publication of his first book of sonnets, *Notebook 1967-68*, a number of Lowell's avowedly loose, wide-ranging translations of classical and European authors were collected in his volume *Imitations*. In it he aims, as he explains, not to produce strict translations but "versions" that he imagines his chosen poets would have produced were they his contemporaries—though in practice he often seems to revise them as though they were his own. Imitation, in short, becomes appropriation.

During this period Lowell also wrote *The Old Glory*, which comprises three plays, *Endicott and the Red Cross; My Kinsman, Major Molineux;* and *Benito Cereno.* The first two are adaptations of short stories by Hawthorne; the third is an adaptation of a considerably longer story by Melville. Though Lowell had no evident interest in Emerson, Whitman, or Thoreau, he was naturally drawn to Hawthorne, whose allegories constitute or fall within the final, fading penumbra of Puritanism, and to *Moby Dick,* in which Ahab's quest is both a natural extension of Puritanism and a perversion of it, and is ultimately a presentiment of its passing. It is difficult to imagine Lowell as a dramatist, but his trio of one-act plays garnered good reviews when first performed.

Lowell's tendency to appropriate the work of others, in which all poets indulge, at times becomes quite extreme, as in his rewriting of Bishop's great short story, "In The Village," as a desultory and pointless poem of his own, "The Scream," in *For The Union Dead;* or as in his notorious, almost verbatim transcriptions, his imitations, or rewritings of Hardwick's personal letters, which he incorporated without permission into several of his sonnets.

The obverse side of Lowell as appropriator and rewriter of the works of others is Lowell as chameleon, as shapeshifter, who has slight purchase on his own ego, on a fixed or secure identity, and whose work takes on the tone of others—just as Lowell's speech took on the Southern accent of Tate and Ransom, and as he adapted to and wrote poems that conformed to their New Critical agenda. Interestingly and oddly, Lowell habitually listed Bishop and Tate, who were longtime personal friends, and Williams, whom he came to know more fleetingly, as the three poets who most influenced him—a list that does not, as one might expect, include poetic luminaries from the past. It was as though these three, by dint of proximity, of close contact, almost literally rubbed off on Lowell, coloring his own work.

Most fruitfully, Lowell's poetry occasionally responds to, is in dialogue with, indeed pays homage to the work of others, while at the same time being very much his own. "For the Union Dead" was a response to but hardly an echo of Allen Tate's "Ode to the Confederate Dead." "Skunk Hour" was a response to Bishop's "The Armadillo." One senses that with Lowell, appropriation and imitation allowed him to remain within the fragile circle of his ego while at the same time tentatively venturing out from it. One of the best of Lowell's imitations, that of Rimbaud's "The Seven Year Old Poet," Lowell manages to catch the quick of the spirit of Rimbaud while also sounding like Lowell, as though it were a collaboration between the two.

4.

Before revisiting Lowell's seemingly endless sonnet sequence, I would like to posit a theory, or to pose a question, which I have not seen posited or posed before. I have mentioned the crucial role played by Lowell's psychiatrist Merrill Moore at a vital juncture of his life, and that Moore was not only a psychiatrist but a poet who himself wrote, throughout his life, an interminable series of sonnets. In contradistinction to Lowell's parents' baffled incomprehension of a son who seemed to them not only unhinged but, after his assault on his father, frighteningly violent, Moore provided Lowell with something like unconditional love. He was the first figure in Lowell's life who recognized in him a poetic genius in the making. It was his intervention that resulted in Lowell's providential escape from Boston, from Harvard, and from his parental milieu, and in his pivotal association with Tate and Ransom who, like Moore, recognized and nurtured his genius. Could Lowell's own almost endless series of sonnets have been an unconscious homage to Moore?

Looking from a more mature vantage point, I find myself, though not altering my view of the weaknesses of Lowell's sonnets, capable of seeing them in a more charitable light. By the time Lowell began his sonnet sequence in his early fifties, he had been subject to multiple rounds of electroshock therapy, to massive doses of Thorazine, and to the ravages of years of alcoholism—in short, to multiple insults to his brain, which perhaps contributed to the fractured, halting, distracted, formally unsuccessful nature of the poems. However, if his sonnets do not succeed as poetic documents, they do succeed, intermittently, simply as human documents.

In my earlier treatment of Lowell's sonnets, I faulted his use of the word "plot" in his "Afterthought" to *Notebook 1967-68* and remarked on his abandonment, after his second book, of straightforward narrative. In this lack of interest in or incapacity for conventional narrative, Lowell, to be fair, was hardly alone. Virtually every twentieth-century poet of real stature who wished to write long poems, and specifically who wished to write poems of epic scope, composed what are in fact congeries of lyrics. Pound's *Cantos*, Crane's *The Bridge*, Olson's *Maximus* poems, and Williams' *Paterson*, to which I would add Berryman's *Dream Songs* and Lowell's *History*, are examples of this trend. Lacking the teleological thrust, they tend to hang together in only a makeshift way and to be subject to the law of diminishing returns.

After *Notebook 1967–68*, an expanded version of which was published in 1970, Lowell published *History* in 1973. Lowell's factual knowledge of history is indeed impressive, even if his static presentation of those facts is not. Most of the sonnets in *History* are brief cameos of historical figures in chronological order. A number of Lowell's literary friends described long, sometimes exhausting discussions with him in which historical and literary figures and their epochs seemed, as previously mentioned, as alive and present to him as anything in the actual present. For the most part, however, Lowell does not quite succeed in making them live on the page.

But it is the Lowell who described himself as "famished for human chances" whom I would most like to highlight here, as this phrase touches upon something I find essential about Lowell's late work. Lowell's sonnet series has something of the promiscuous inclusivity of Whitman's "Song of Myself," though it lacks Whitman's galvanizing instinct for the metaphysical. Lowell seems to me to have almost no natural instinct or affinity for either the metaphysical or the philosophical. He seems every bit as averse to abstraction as Williams, a fact as evident in the strained and ramshackle symbolism of *Lord Weary's Castle* as in his subsequent work. His mind and his discussions of poetry were essentially impressionistic and anecdotal. They were those of an aristocratic magpie flitting associatively among occultly related topoi. He left behind little extended literary criticism of any kind. Yet Lowell's propensity for inclusion seems more humanly grounded than that of any other American poet except Whitman and Williams. Whitman's poems seem always to be working in the spirit of the words uttered by a character in a play by the Roman playwright Terence, "Nothing human is alien to me." Lowell's sonnets seem guided by the notion that "nothing human shall be left unaccounted for by me."

This instinct for inclusion by endless addition was hardly a given for Lowell. It grew over time as his sense of self grew less and less parochial. It is a testament to Lowell's continued openness to and hunger for "human chances," for human connections, even in the face of a traumatic psychic and physical affliction that might have caused him to shut down completely.

Though there is little of the metaphysical in Lowell's work, there is much, again, of the vividly anecdotal. Lowell's poems to an extraordinary degree came to be populated by distinctive human others, even if filtered at times through the distorting prism of abnormal states of consciousness. Instead of shutting down as he grew older and more physically infirm, Lowell somehow managed to allow himself to become more open, more vulnerable, both to others and to his own experiences, as well as more painfully aware of the harm he had done, even if often involuntarily, to others. His transcriptions of his experience, no longer ironically distanced, become painfully raw. All of these trends and others I shall later discuss become touchingly evident in his final book, *Day by Day*, whose poems, regardless of their poetic merit, which is often considerable, are moving human testaments.

History concludes with Lowell's poetic versions of dispatches from the trenches, a record of his engagement with the civil rights and anti-war movements of the late sixties, including accounts of the famous march on the Pentagon in which he participated. Lowell was cultivating a political awareness that, breaking through the circle of his concern with his own suffering, included an awakened consciousness of the suffering of others.

Norman Mailer's remarkable book *Armies of the Night* contains a number of passages on Lowell that proffer a strikingly vivid portrait of the poet as unlikely agent provocateur. Lowell's daughter Harriet has said that of all those who have written on Lowell, Mailer comes the closest to describing the father she knew as a child. Mailer regards Lowell with something of the amused, bemused, ironical tone that Lowell at times adopts toward himself. Mailer's portrait of Lowell, never condescending, always affectionate, describes a Lowell who is myopic, abstracted, often seemingly befuddled or nonplussed by being part of the moil of an indifferent crowd, but who nonetheless, despite himself, retains the air of an aristocrat, seeming, in Whitman's words, to be both in the game and out of it. He also, however, seemed intent on learning how to adapt himself to a milieu that was for him unfamiliar.

Finally, although there is no historical tropism in Lowell's sonnets, no sense, as in *Lord Weary's Castle*, or even as in the title poem of *For the Union Dead* with its preoccupation with nuclear annihilation, of history moving toward some apocalyptic end, there *is* perhaps what might be called a biological tropism increasingly at work in Lowell's sonnets. Surely Lowell grew more aware, as his sonnet sequence continued, that his alcoholism, his lifetime of chain smoking, and the series of shocks, natural and unnatural, that his flesh had been heir to, weakening his heart, presaged an early death. Paradoxically, it was this presentiment that his days were numbered that perhaps led him, somewhat desperately, to be "famished for human chances," chances whose embrace signaled an intense commitment to life. What can seem like mere temporizing in Lowell's sonnets—including his propensity for endless revision, his reluctance to view his sonnets individually or as a whole as finished—perhaps, as by a kind of magical thinking, seemed to serve him as a stay against the inevitability of encroaching death.

5.

I confess that one of the minor functions I would like the several essays in this section of the book to perform is to redress the current imbalance between Lowell's and Bishop's reputations. It is now almost as unjust as the critical subordination of Bishop to Lowell during their lifetimes.

I still regard Bishop as the finest poet of her generation. With typical self-deprecation that conceals, at the same time, a not-entirely-humble self-regard, Bishop once referred to herself as "a minor Wordsworth." I consider her, as she considered herself, as at least in part a Neo-Romantic. I feel more naturally drawn to her work than to Lowell's. If I were merely following my own predilections, I should be writing about her here. But much, and much that has been cogent and insightful, has already been and continues to be written about Bishop.

Bishop was not one who tended, with rare exceptions, to open herself up to others. The reasons for this, rooted in a harrowing childhood and tragedies in her adult life, foremost among them the suicide of her longtime lover, Lota de Macedo Soares, are entirely understandable. No doubt the potential stigma of being seen as gay accounts for the lack of any trace in her work, with the exception of one of her slightest poems, "The Shampoo," of her thirteen-year-long love affair with Lota, a brilliant, politically connected, at times manically energetic, Brazilian aristocrat who built an idyllic retreat for herself and Bishop an hour outside of Rio. It was to become, in a sense, Bishop's first and only true home.

In general, Bishop's default reaction to others seemed to me not simply one of reticence but also of disapproval. In her extraordinary poem "In The Waiting Room," which is about her first coming to awareness of herself at five years old as an "I," as a separate person, she notes, upon hearing her aunt's cry of pain during a visit to the dentist, "even then I knew she was / a foolish, timid woman."

Bishop, who suffered from various ailments, most prominently from asthma, was physically and emotionally fragile, easily overwhelmed, and perhaps that very fragility led to her toughness. She could be cold and subtly intimidating in her demeanor toward others. In the poetry workshop I took with her, all of her students were required to write a critical paper on one of a list of six or seven contemporary poets she handed out to us. I chose to write on Berryman. In my one face-to-face meeting with Bishop, it became clear that she regarded my choice of Berryman as an unfortunate one. I felt as though I had been caught out, my judgement revealed as defective. Certainly I had been guilty of over-praising Berryman's poems, which, uniquely among those of the poets of his generation, had influenced my own fledgling work. Though I admired Bishop's relatively pristine poems more, perhaps because they had a kind of sealed-off self-sufficiency, intimidating in their near perfection, I found Berryman's works, and particularly his syncopated rhythms, of more use to me.

Later I heard that Bishop had very much disapproved of Berryman's occasional alcoholic rampages at dinner parties they had both attended years earlier. Berryman often grew raucously contentious at such affairs and made passes at men as well as women. Bishop, too, was an alcoholic, but a discreet one. Berryman's poems, with their sexual frankness, with their lexical extravagance, with their odd patois and wrenching of syntax, were perhaps likewise deemed by her deplorably indecorous. I was left to wonder why Bishop had included Berryman's name on the list at all.

How different was my sole, still briefer, one-on-one encounter with Lowell himself! As I was ascending, one afternoon, from the second to the third story of Harvard's Lamont Library, I heard the sound of lumbering footsteps directly behind me. As I held open the door to the third floor to let this apparently clumsy figure through, I turned around and was startled to find myself face-to-face with Lowell, who was wearing a rumpled, lime-green sports coat. His long grey hair, a sign of solidarity with my generation, straggled almost to his shoulders. He looked as though he had just gotten out of bed after having slept all night in his clothes. And yet he was an imposing presence. Looking me directly in the eye for what seemed a good three or four seconds, he said, "Thank you," with real feeling, as though I had performed for him a gallant service. That silent look, accompanied by two words, was somehow, I liked, albeit absurdly, to think, more eloquent than the many words I would have heard had Lowell admitted me into his poetry workshop.

I long harbored another distinct memory, or what I regarded as a distinct memory, of Lowell. I recalled attending the first day of Lowell's spring semester seminar on fiction. Lowell entered the classroom slightly late. He appeared to be agitated. Apparently, he had absent-mindedly left his briefcase, which contained all of the notes that he had prepared for the class, in the taxi that had conveyed him to this, his appointed destination. Outside, it was an unseasonably sweltering day. The classroom was hot and stuffy. Lowell asked a student to open a window. The lawn adjoining classroom was being mowed by an exceptionally loud lawnmower. Lowell declared, half-jokingly, still appearing flustered and embarrassed, that we had two alternatives—either to close the window and perish of heatstroke, or to leave it open and be unable to hear a word of what he would be saying.

I don't recall how this conundrum was resolved. I do recall returning to the same classroom the following week. A notice was taped to the door to inform us that the class had been cancelled. We all knew what this meant. Lowell was doubtless back for another stint at McLean's Hospital.

We know now, of course, that memory is notoriously unreliable. It is almost never, if ever, a faithful copy or transcript of our experience. It is often as much imagined as recalled. Sometimes particular memories are even entirely imagined when something about their vividness convinces us they are true.

Upon later reflection, it occurred to me that this formerly unquestioned, putative memory of mine was woven by me out of whole cloth. The beginning of the spring semester at Harvard does not mean that spring has arrived. It seems highly unlikely that such an unseasonably sweltering day could have occurred in early March, or that there would have been much of a lawn outside to be mowed.

From whence had this memory arisen? Perhaps from a dream, a wish fulfillment. I had attended one of Lowell's classes after all! Perhaps, to paraphrase one of Keats' remarks on the imagination, it was a dream from which I awoke and due to its preternatural vividness eventually came to consider true.

6.

Before turning to Lowell's last book, *Day by Day*, I want to cast yet another retrospective glance, this time at a younger contemporary of Lowell's, at a poet who had a more than merely tangential relationship to him. I am referring to Allen Ginsberg, whose "Howl," like Lowell's *For the Union Dead*, constitutes a rare instance of a successful American political poem. Both Lowell and Ginsberg are estimable poets whose stars have fallen since their deaths, and both are ripe for a critical reappraisal.

The work of the Beats was at least equally scandalous as the initially scandalous avatars of the confessional school, but because they were not regarded as a part of the official culture of the time or scarcely of any culture at all, they were safely ignored, if not by the police then by poetic academicians. Kerouac's *On The Road*, notoriously fueled by a three-day Benzedrine high, valorized the aimless escapades of those drifting in the shadows of what Lowell called the "tranquilized fifties." Burroughs, from *Naked Lunch* on, not only chronicled but perversely championed the depredations of heroin addiction. In one notorious incident, he killed his wife by attempting to shoot an apple off her head.

It was Allen Ginsberg, of course, who was both the impresario and the preeminent bard of the Beats. Lowell, unlike his fellow academic poets and the critics who supported them, had the sense to realize he had something to learn from Ginsberg, with whom he participated in several joint readings over the years. Ginsberg was in fact very much a man of culture, of almost rabbinical learning, and the two men clearly felt an affinity for each other. Perhaps Lowell chatted with Ginsberg about his distinguished Jewish forebear, Mordecai Meyers, of whom he was particularly proud.

Ginsberg was in effect a confessional poet before the fact. And yet his greatest poems, "Howl" and his harrowing masterpiece "Kaddish," unlike most of those typically associated with the confessional school, manage, like "Skunk Hour," "For the Union Dead," and "Waking Early Sunday Morning," to transcend the confines of the merely personal.

"Howl" is a rhetorical tour de force, but "Kaddish," an extraordinarily compassionate, clear-sighted, and unflinching poem on his mother, Naomi, is Ginsberg's masterpiece. Naomi, a paranoid schizophrenic, was shepherded by her pubescent son in and out of a state mental hospital in New Jersey, a role Ginsberg's father felt unable to assume, until she finally was warehoused there for good. In "Kaddish," also written in Biblical cadences, Naomi's naked, scarred, and deteriorating body, including the wens on her breast and her "bearded vagina," which is rendered in excruciating detail, becomes a palimpsest that has been defaced by a society that has objectified and discarded it. Of course, there is something scandalous, or apparently scandalous, in Ginsberg's more than frank treatment of his mother's body. In "Kaddish," the agony of the mother is given voice by the anguished cries of the son.

The degree to which the psychiatric establishment, from the nineteenth and well into the twentieth century, brutalized women's bodies—not only those of schizophrenics, but those merely deemed "hysterical"—by subjecting them to barbarous cures, is perhaps too little known. Freud himself sought to cure female "hysterics" by subjecting their reproductive organs to painful and sterilizing doses of radiation. If "Kaddish" has not been taken up by feminist theorists, it certainly should be. It opens a door to the horrors of state mental institutions, horrors that most of us would prefer not to witness.

Finally, there is a further political dimension to "Kaddish." Before descending into madness, Naomi, as the poem recounts, had affiliated herself with the Communist party. Though later her political views assumed the form of paranoid fantasies, her engagement with the Communist party was the precursor of her son's later radicalism.

Ginsberg aligned himself with a prophetic tradition that rescues his poems from being too merely personal. Ginsberg was America's first great Jewish, or Jewish/Buddhist, poet. The cadences of his poetry reflect the syntactic parallelism of the Biblical prophets and psalmists as well as that of the similarly inspired Christopher Smart, Blake, and Whitman.

Ginsberg undertook multiple vocations: that of the poet; that of the prophet; that of the disciple of his Tibetan Buddhist guru; that of the precursor and later that of the advocate for what came too optimistically to be called the New Age; that of the pioneer in being fully open and frank about his homosexuality, an unsung hero of what would later become the gay rights movement; that of mythographer of the Beat Generation; and finally that of a fully engaged and remarkably well-informed political advocate for the marginal and disenfranchised in the United States and throughout the world. In short, despite his human and poetic flaws, he lived a life of unstinting generosity.

Lowell, like Ginsberg, had once assumed a prophetic role, one that, as it turned out, was the product of a protracted manic high, and that was no longer tenable when that high waned. Ginsberg's assumption of such a role, which he never abandoned, was inaugurated by an auditory hallucination of William Blake reading "Ah! Sun-flower" and "The Sick Rose." In the aftermath of this experience, which lasted several days, Ginsberg had an intense experience of the interconnectedness of all things, which he described as "a sudden awakening into a totally deeper real universe than I'd been existing in."

There is a kind of morphological similarity between the hallucinations of psychotics and the visions of mystics. How does one differentiate between the two? Most psychiatrists regard all such experiences as pathological and are therefore, for the purposes of this discussion, beside the point. Of course, there is no surefire test to differentiate between profoundly transformative visionary states and pathological ones, but genuine mystics tend to lead productive lives that are an ongoing testament to a sanity that is deeper, more encompassing, and more spontaneous than that which most societies deem to be sane.

After having survived a traumatic childhood and youth that could have permanently derailed many, Ginsberg, by his mid-twenties, seemed to have found himself. Despite being regarded by some as a kind of New Age wild man, he was preeminently nothing if not sane, was a survivor who did far more than merely survive, but rather lived an extraordinarily committed and productive life.

Though Lowell's destructive behavior when manic led him to question a moral authority he had once too glibly assumed, he never ceased to indict, though in a vexed, troubled, and often self-doubting way, a society that equated money with power, and power with an increasingly imperial violence. Like Ginsberg, he was an active opponent of the Vietnam War. Also like Ginsberg, he overcame daunting obstacles and led, ultimately, at least as a poet, a prolifically productive life.

Ginsberg, like Bishop and Lowell, died too young—in his case at the relatively premature age of seventy. Ginsberg had long had health problems. He had had two minor strokes, originally misdiagnosed as Bell's Palsy, in the '70s, leaving one side of his face partly paralyzed. A lifelong smoker, he also suffered from high blood pressure and increasingly severe heart problems. Nonetheless, he did not cut back on his frenetic schedule until the last several months of his life. Even then, he continued to write and to bail out friends who were in financial difficulty. In the last days of his life, he was surrounded around the clock by rotating convoys of friends, and by the sounds of the live chanting of mantras, a practice that had long been integral to his spiritual life. He died of liver cancer in 1997. By that time his fame, or his notoriety, at least in his own country, had long since been on the wane.

Upon his death, Helen Vendler wrote an elegy, or eulogy, in the form of extraordinarily passionate and heartfelt encomium not only to Ginsburg as a poet whom she felt had not gotten his critical due but as a man whom she considered a friend, although one whom she wished she had visited more often. She wrote that both Ginsberg's life and work had granted her and many of her generation the license, indeed the freedom and courage, to aspire to be their truest and most authentic selves.

One of Lowell's last readings was a joint reading with Ginsberg in 1977 at St. Marks-in-the-Bowery in New York, a venue that had long been hospitable to both avant-garde and politically engaged poetry. As one listens to the tape of that reading, Ginsberg, who reads first, seems very much in command, repeatedly and attentively testing to make sure that the microphone he and Lowell will share is in full working order, and insisting that all the members of the audience are settled quietly in their seats before the reading begins. He is neither whimsical nor humorous, but serious and authoritative. He then proceeds to read with his arresting baritone voice, a remarkable and commanding vocal instrument.

Among the poems he reads is a moving and painful account of his father's death, which once again does not spare the reader a frank account of the old man's physical decline. The plangent title of this group of poems, *Don't Grow Old,* from which Ginsberg reads excerpts, sounds as if it could have been written by Lowell. It seems to me that Ginsberg's reading of these poems was a tacit and touching tribute to Lowell, whom Ginsberg knew to be in seriously ill health.

Lowell, who reads next, charms and seduces rather than overpowers the audience, making a series of wry remarks that draw considerable laughter. After praising Ginsberg's poem "Kaddish" as a masterpiece, Lowell remarks that he disagrees with critics who place him and Ginsberg, to whom he refers, with evident affection, as "Allen," at opposite ends of the poetic spectrum. He proclaims, with his considerable gift for the aphoristic, "Allen and I are at opposite ends of William

Carlos Williams," a remark that is met with hearty laughter. He notes the personal relationship that both he and Allen were blessed to have had with Williams. It seems to me that this seemingly odd nexus—Ginsberg/ Williams/ Lowell—has been too little remarked upon.

At first Lowell, who has some difficulty in shuffling through his poems to find those he intends to read, seems, unlike Ginsberg, far from in command. When he begins to read, however, he rises to the occasion and recites his poems with a rhetorical force almost equal to that of Ginsberg. One thinks of St. Marks-in-the-Bowery as a milieu that would have been more sympathetic to Ginsberg than to Lowell, but the audience seems to know many of Lowell's poems almost by heart and applauds, without missing a beat, upon their conclusions. Gregory Corso, a Beat poet who was as notable for his eccentric, flamboyant high jinks as for his poetry, can even be heard in the background complaining that Lowell has skipped a line in his reading of "Man and Wife." Lowell wryly says, "Point taken," then concludes by reading a meditation on Odysseus that would appear later as the first poem in *Day by Day*.

Listening to the reading is like overhearing a pair of lions roaring. One is already, at fifty, past his prime. The other is nearing his end. The listener is startled by the clear sense conveyed of the kinship between the two men.

7.

Freed from the strait-jacket of the unrhymed sonnet, the poems of *Day by Day* are once again able to breathe, to dilate, to expand or contract according to the poet's well-honed instinct. Many of these poems, perhaps more than ever in Lowell's poetry, seem to flow, even if discontinuously, obeying their own whims, following their own idiosyncratic course, including at times a number of false starts, deflections, and interruptions.

Day by Day is nothing if not a book of memory. In my youth, as previously discussed, I deemed the muse of memory inferior to what Blake calls the "Poetic Genius," akin to Coleridge's primary and secondary imagination. Blake's "muse of memory" is essentially synonymous with Coleridge's derogatory term "fancy." To use Lowell's terms, I preferred the "imagined" to the "recalled." It is, I suppose, time or past time to give Mnemosyne, the muse of memory, her due. And perhaps to recognize that she and the Poetic Genius can walk hand in hand. My earlier, brief account of a memory of Lowell that turned out to be entirely imagined was intended as a parable, a precursor to my discussion here.

The poems of *Day by Day* are written by a man who, now suffering from congestive heart failure, is fully conscious, although he is in his late fifties, that he is dying. They are therefore poems of old age, of a time when the instinct to recall, to look back, becomes something like an imperative. They are, I think, among those poems of old age in which it is evident that the poet is still evolving and growing. The poems in *Day by Day* constitute a late flowering of Lowell's poetic genius and evince the transformative power of the imaginative working in concert with the retrospective.

William Carlos Williams, similarly afflicted physically and psychically in his later years after having experienced a series of debilitating strokes, his once-keen senses and easy access to words no longer readily available, wrote in his extraordinary poem "The Descent":

> ...
>
> Memory is a kind
> of accomplishment
> a sort of renewal
> even
> an initiation, since the spaces it opens are new places
> inhabited by hordes
> heretofore unrealized
> of new kinds—
> since their movements
> are toward new objectives
> (even though formerly they were abandoned)

Memory as "initiation." Opening "new places." New places of "new kinds." Moving toward objectives "formerly... abandoned." Even for Williams, previously committed to a poetry of the pure percept, memory functions in this poem much as we would hope the imagination does.

Remarkably, Lowell wrote late in his life that he was grateful for some of his most extreme and harrowing experiences. They opened spaces that would have otherwise been unrealized. Their darkness, too, when accepted, Lowell wrote, was in some way beautiful. This stance, again, is similar to what in Hinduism and Buddhism is called tantra, in which all experiences, even the most transgressive and apparently horrifying, are neither to be desired nor, more importantly, to be shunned, and in which all finally are experienced, when fully and unreservedly accepted, as blissful, as beautiful.

Day by Day revisits various periods of Lowell's past and the various figures associated with them. Chief among these figures are his parents, particularly his mother; friends, such as Frank Parker, from prep school; and some of his poetic peers, including John Berryman, to whom he felt increasingly close as he grew older and about whom he writes, in *Day by Day*, in several touching poems. Typically, he returns to these figures in a spirit of kinship and solidarity. Where appropriate, he offers them forgiveness and absolution while at the same time making amends, himself seeking forgiveness. The ending of one of many poems to his mother in *Day by Day* is typical: "It has taken me the time since you died / to discover that you are as human as I am /...if I am."

But *Day by Day* is not only a book of memory. It addresses the present as well with a new sense of urgency. I have written earlier about a stanza from "Waking Early Sunday Morning" as an example of a strain of sensuousness in Lowell's poetry that is often overlooked. That sensuousness is often startlingly evident in these poems, which encompass both the sensual and the explicitly sexual. Subsequent to *Lord Weary's Castle,* there had long been an appreciation of eros in Lowell's poetry. In a number of poems in *Day by Day,* it comes to the fore. At the same time, there has long been a connection in Western poetry between the erotic and the elegiac, which also is fully present here in a number of poems that have a kind of burnished glow.

Lowell writes in *Day by Day* that he feels like a turtle without a shell, without any protective carapace. His vulnerability, his often-painful openness to experience, became more pronounced as he aged. Yet his hunger "for human chances" remained, in periods of recovery, fully intact, as did his powerful, unshakeable sense of his vocation as a poet. He, of course, never abandoned writing poems, but here more than ever, they become self-evidently perhaps the chief among the benign tethers that tie Lowell to life. They are his allies in what has become a quest to survive. The disjunction between art and life had never been a feature of Lowell's poetry. In *Day by Day*, they seem almost fully aligned.

Finally, and perhaps most harrowingly and most touchingly, the poems once again track, now as it were in real time, the terrible internal seasons of Lowell's mental illness, the oscillation between periods of madness and periods of an often slow and tentative recovery. This oscillation grew more exhausting as Lowell grew older. The pole of madness is represented most powerfully in *Day by Day* in an extraordinary series of poems including "Home," "Shadow," and "Notice," toward the end of the book. Lowell's bemused, patrician irony, his detachment from the horror of certain of his experiences, is now a thing of the past. Just as his dispatches from hell have a new directness, urgency, and immediacy, so his depictions of blessed periods of recovery have an added poignance.

Trying to decide which poems from *Day by Day* about which to write has involved a painful and ultimately to some degree an arbitrary choice. I have decided to focus on three poems that appear toward the end of the book, after the aforementioned dispatches from hell: "Shifting Colors," "The Downlook," and the last poem in the book, "Epilogue."

Neither of the first two of these poems, I should point out, are perfectly realized. As in Lowell's sonnets, neither seems to carry a single energetic impulse from start to finish. Both, but particularly the second, "The Downlook," proceed by odd, disjunctive, private, associative or dissociative leaps. But what were flaws in the case of the sonnets, when given more ample room, and when we surrender to the strange movement of the poems, give us a glimpse into a kind of new poetic world. Again, when our understanding is balked, and we submit to the poems' disjunctive movement, difficult to identify but nonetheless powerful feelings are stirred up, feelings that are like colors that are slightly different from any we have yet seen. None of these poems is a mere transcription of things seen or pictures copied verbatim from scenes stored in memory. In their own way, they are evidence of things unseen. In their own way, they are imaginative exercises. I cite the first of these poems below.

SHIFTING COLORS

I fish until the clouds turn blue,
weary of self-torture, ready to paint
lilacs or confuse a thousand leaves,
as landscapists must.

My eye returns to my double,
an ageless big white horse,
slightly discolored by dirt
cropping the green shelf diagonal
to the artificial troutpond—
unmoving, it shifts as I move,
and works the whole field in the course of a day.

Poor measured, neurotic man—
animals are more instinctive virtuosi.

Ducks splash deceptively like fish;
fish break water with the wings of a bird to escape.

A hissing goose sways in stationary anger;
purple bluebells rise in ledges on the lake.

A single cuckoo gifted with a pregnant word
shifts like the sun from wood to wood.

All day my miscast troutfly buzzes about my ears
and empty mind.

But nature is sundrunk with sex—
how could a man fail to notice, man
the one pornographer among the animals?

I seek leave unimpassioned by my body,
I am too weak to strain to remember, or give
recollection the eye of the microscope. I see
horse and meadow, duck and pond,
universal consolatory
description without significance,
transcribed verbatim by my eye.

This is not the directness that catches
everything on the run and then expires—
I would write only in response to the gods,
like Mallarmé who had the good fortune
to find a style that made writing impossible.

In Elizabeth Bishop's finest poems, description becomes revelation. In her famous poem "At the Fish Houses," and in a number of other poems, the apparently continuous and mimetic suddenly shifts gears and becomes visionary. "Shifting Colors" gives the lie to Lowell's own self-characterization, in the poem itself, of his work as being mere "description without significance / transcribed verbatim by my eye." I would contend, to the contrary, that in "Shifting Colors" apparently mimetic description becomes, in its own way, revelation.

Fishing, in this poem and in others, is a trope for writing, which for Lowell involves an escape from "self-torture." The poet, whose mind is blessedly "empty," casts his fly all day, surrounded by a nature that is apprehended as shifting, dynamic, alive, as is suggested by the five couplets that constitute the third to the seventh of the poem's highly irregular stanzas. The poet/speaker's fly buzzes about his ears as though it has been transformed into an actual fly. The poem's metamorphoses are worthy of Ovid. Lowell's depictions of the scene around him are sensuous, are open to, and keenly register, the shifting colors of the natural world, and end with the revelation that nature is "sundrunk with sex." The last, late flowering of the erotic in all of its senses that characterizes *Day by Day* is abundantly in evidence here.

The charmingly metamorphic couplet on ducks who descend and, in splashing on the surface of the water, mirror fish who break its surface as they fly upward, is reminiscent of the many amphibious and underwater creatures who crop up regularly in his poetry and who, like Lowell—an "undersea fellow" with an affinity to the "kingdom of the fish and reptile"—are shape-shifters. Lowell would have known that he was born under the sign of Pisces, the fish. One thinks of the poem in *Day by Day* entitled "Turtles," in this case snapping turtles, mostly subaqueous creatures whose powerful jaws can cause grave harm to unwary swimmers; and one recalls, too, Lowell's earlier reference to himself as a turtle without a shell. He manages to identify with snapping turtles and therefore does not fear them. He, like them, is a swimmer, and water is his element.

In "Shifting Colors," the poet identifies as well with a white horse, who, although unlike Lowell in being "ageless," is like him busy at work all day cropping a nearby field while Lowell fishes for what lies beneath the pond's surface. The suggestion here is that Lowell, like his "double," is not always a "measured, neurotic man," but also an "instinctive virtuoso," and that he, too, is an animal among animals, an embodied being who cannot willfully escape from the body even as it is failing.

While grounded in the physical, the poem is also self-consciously aware of its status as art. The poet/speaker immediately likens himself to a painter, to a landscapist, invoking the classical tradition, *ut pictura poesis*, that likens painting and poetry as mimetic art forms, an affinity that has given rise to countless ekphrastic poems. The poet, after all, is fishing in an "artificial" pond whose status is later arbitrarily upgraded to that of a "lake." Is Lowell's art, as he seems to suggest, simply mimetic, or is something, as I am suggesting, more than the shallow illusion of the merely mimetic at play in it?

The poet/landscapist/fisher/horse, a kind of compound subject, has/have been at work all day. Presumably, night is soon to follow. The poet, exhausted, nearing death, seeks leave both of a too-impassioned body, one that is perhaps too frail to consummate its desires, just as it is "too weak" to write, to remember, an activity that Lowell characterizes as involving straining to "give / recollection the eye of the microscope."

Once again, Lowell is representing his art as entirely beholden to the muse of memory and to a pointless, microscopically mimetic transcription not only of what happens but of what has already happened. Such art lacks (in a phrase that once again puns on the word "fly") "the directness that catches everything on the fly," that requires that the poet be alert and rooted in the present.

This characterization may be more nearly accurate with respect to the weaker of Lowell's later poems, but it is not true of "Shifting Colors," in which Lowell is indeed, in Blake's words, "kissing the moment as it flies," is keenly alert, as in the couplets I have cited, to nature's shifting colors, to her constant interstitial moments of transition, to a dynamism that is ever-changing. Here, alert and present, Lowell's eye indeed catches everything on the fly, in living motion.

And yet the poet/speaker, more than ever before subject to exhaustion, longs to take leave both of his body and of the exigencies of art, and as a result entertains a kind of false alternative to his aesthetic. He aspires to the status of Mallarmé, that most disembodied and hieratic of poets, who has had "the good fortune to find a style that makes writing impossible." Lowell wishes, he claims, to write only in response to the gods, to be spurred by and answerable to some vital source that at the same time provides a kind of metaphysical sanction.

But Lowell could scarcely be less like Mallarmé. Nor is he a Romantic poet, seeking, or believing in, the gods or some other metaphysical entity or force once thought to be the wellspring of poetry. Nor, finally, does he ultimately wish, despite the fatigue and strain entailed by the writing of poems, to find a style that makes writing impossible, because writing poetry is vitally connected with his own still-urgent wish to survive, his determination not to simply succumb, like so many of the poets of his generation, to the allure of death.

"Shifting Colors" is hardly naively mimetic, representing a scene merely copied, transcribed verbatim by the eye. Lowell's mature art, though grounded in the mimetic, in accuracy of perception, though rooted in memory, at its best walks hand in hand with the mysterious, with the unaccountable, and touches something close to the quick of what Coleridge called the imaginative. The boundary between the imagined and the recalled, between that which is freshly perceived in the present and the moment in which it is transcribed after the fact, begins to dissolve. When one asks questions of "Shifting Colors," it provides answers quite different from those seemingly supplied by the poem itself.

The second of my chosen poems, "The Downlook," seems initially at least to be written in the present tense but is in fact written under the aegis of the muse of memory.

THE DOWNLOOK

> For the last two minutes, the retiring monarchy
> of the full moon looks down on the first chirping sparrows—
> nothing lovelier than waking to find
> another breathing body in my bed...
> glowshadow halfcovered with dayclothes like my own,
> caught in my arms.
>
> Last summer nothing dared impede
> the flow of the body's thousand rivulets of welcome,
> winding effortlessly, but with ambiguous invention—
> safety in nearness.
>
> Now the downlook, the downlook—small fuss,
> nothing that could earn a line or picture
> in the responsible daily paper we'll be reading,
> an anthology of the unredeemable world
> beyond the accumulative genius of prose or this—
> a day that sharpens apprehension by dulling;
> each miss must be a mile,

if one risk the narrow two-lane highway.

It's impotence and impertinence to ask directions,
while staring right and left in two-way traffic.

There's no greater happiness in days of the downlook
than to turn back to recapture former joy.

Ah loved perhaps before I knew you,
others have been lost like this,
yet found foothold
by winning the dolphin from the humming water.

How often have my antics
and insupportable, trespassing tongue
gone astray and led me to prison . . .
to lying . . . kneeling . . . standing.

The first two stanzas of the poem, technically an aubade, a poem in celebration of waking with a beloved other, are a kind of sonorous triumph of Lowell's rhetoric at its best, as is the whole poem if one reads it merely for sound, not for sense. Its rhythm somehow reminds me of Hart Crane's beautiful, likewise mysterious poem "Repose of Rivers."

Immediately after the first two stanzas, it becomes clear that what seems to be unfolding vividly in the present tense is in fact being remembered by a speaker who is now in far more straitened circumstances, standing as though paralyzed in the middle of a highway with traffic moving both ways, not even willing to risk the "impertinence" of asking for directions. The rhetoric of the remainder of the poem becomes radically disjunctive, leaping from one brief stanza to the next, the connections not always clear, the thought, again, seemingly disorganized yet felt by this reader, at least, to be occultly related.

What is meant by the neologism "downlook?" It is avowedly a look backward in time to a happier era but also perhaps a look backward in space, like the backward looks of Orpheus and Lot, both of which led to the loss of a beloved wife, analogous in this case to Lowell's estrangement from the last of his three wives, the brilliant and beautiful English novelist Lady Caroline Blackwood. It is also perhaps, quite literally, a look downward, as though in shame or contrition, into a kind of abyss.

In Lowell's private symbolism, the dolphin, yet another amphibious creature, refers to Blackwood, an overwhelmingly attractive but also dangerous Circe. Lowell had an affair with her, then married her, thus scandalously abandoning, as previously discussed, his extraordinarily loyal second wife, Elizabeth Hardwick, and their daughter Harriet. Lowell's passionate but ultimately disastrous and unsustainable marriage to Lady Caroline, an alcoholic who was in her own way as unstable as Lowell himself, had finally come apart, leaving Lowell in a kind of limbo, or what at times felt like hell itself, from which most of the poems in *Day by Day* are written. Here he looks back toward the moment at which he first won Lady Caroline from the "humming water"—as others, alas, have before him.

The poem's last stanza seems particularly unexpected, disjunctive:

> How often have my antics
> and insupportable, trespassing tongue
> gone astray and led me to prison...
> to lying... kneeling... standing.

The poem's concluding line is a stutter of ellipses. The stanza as a whole reflects a powerful strain of remorse and self-indictment that runs throughout the entire book, occasioning Lowell's need to forgive others, chiefly his parents, their trespasses, and to make amends for his own, seeking absolution. The book contains many genuinely confessional moments, moments that have, for the first time in Lowell's work, the feeling of an authentic spirituality. The last line of the poem, with its sequence of three words—of "lying" in its double sense of telling lies and of being in a literally fallen state; followed by "kneeling," as though in prayer; and finally by "standing," which seems to hint at the possibility of regeneration—reflects not only a mature spirituality but also the reiterated cycles of mental disintegration and recovery that were characteristic of a life blighted by an illness that occasioned Lowell's repeated experiences of suffering and renewal.

However one interprets or fails to interpret this poem, it too clearly embodies not only the simply recalled but also the vitally imagined.

Finally, I will end where Lowell's work quite literally ends, with his poem "Epilogue," which in its own way seems to attain, like "For the Union Dead," if more modestly, a kind of perfection.

Many of the poems of *Day by Day*, particularly the many poems on his mother and on the central trauma of his life—his knowledge of having been an unwanted child—are engaged in a touching, ongoing struggle for a kind of Freudian self-knowledge that seems, as ever, elusive. And yet "Epilogue," which has come to serve informally as Lowell's epitaph—one of many composed by English writers, from Keats to Yeats, for themselves—does reflect a remarkably clear-eyed self-knowledge, particularly regarding the nature of his art, which was the central and abiding concern of his life, ultimately trumping all others.

EPILOGUE

Those blessèd structures, plot and rhyme—
why are they of no use to me now
I want to make
something imagined, not recalled?
I hear the noise of my own voice:
the painter's vision is not a lens,
it trembles to caress the light.
But sometimes everything I write
with the threadbare art of my eye
seems a snapshot,
lurid, rapid, garish, grouped,
heightened from life,
yet paralyzed by fact.
All's misalliance.
Yet why not say what happened?
Pray for the grace of accuracy
Vermeer gave to the sun's illumination
stealing like the tide across a map
to his girl solid with yearning.
We are poor passing facts,
warned by that to give
each figure in the photograph
his living name.

It would take a stone heart for anyone with any knowledge of Lowell's life or art not to be moved by this poem. I hope much that I have already written serves as a kind of commentary or gloss on the poem: the wish to write something imagined, not recalled; the recognition that the mimetic nature of his art allies him with poets and painters and, more radically, with photographers, in what is yet another ekphrastic poem; the entirely characteristic clustering of not three but here four adjectives to describe his poems; the fear that his work, unlike life, is static, paralyzed by fact. And so on. But I wish here simply to note the extraordinary tenderness and delicacy of this poem by a poet who had perhaps too often succumbed in the past to a kind of violent rhetoric. Here, as in so many of Lowell's poems, the sun and its light is linked with eros. Touchingly, the painter's vision "trembles to caress the light," an impossibility in the world of fact but not in the world of metaphor.

I want especially acknowledge the beauty and power of the poem's last lines. The poet exhorts himself to "pray" for "grace," in this case for Vermeer's "grace of accuracy" in registering "the sun's illumination / stealing like the tide across a map /

to his girl solid with yearning." The poem moves from "misalliance" to a powerful alignment of life and art. Surely, yet again, these lines have the incandescence of something imagined, not simply recalled. The poem's final four lines, particularly the acknowledgment that we are all "poor passing facts," reminds me of Shakespeare's tragedies, and particularly of the recognition in *King Lear* that we are all at base "bare, forked animals," solitary creatures subject to insults both psychic and physical as we inevitably move toward death and oblivion. In the face of this evanescence, it is the task of the poet "to give / each figure in the photograph / his living name." Not just a name, but a living, perhaps even somehow a redeemed name. The whole poem is a prayer. It is a prayer for all of us as poor passing facts, as vulnerable creatures, and above all, simply as human.

It occurs to me now, finally, that I need to make amends, to ask Lowell himself for forgiveness and absolution, for my own youthful indictment of him as trading strategically on his family name, for projecting the ambivalence of my own somewhat more orderly mind on Lowell's at times magnificently disorderly one. For being, in effect, a kind of hanging judge. Lowell was too engrossed in the vicissitudes of grappling with madness, with making some sense of chaos, to have engaged in such cunning stratagems.

Finally I, too, like Lowell, have often descended into my own kind of terrifying madness. I will make my own confession here: even as I have written this, I have been submerged in such a state, one from which I see little hope, at my age, of emerging. I fear that I, too, in advance, need to pray for absolution and forgiveness for whatever pain my state might have caused others and for whatever greater pain it might still cause them. As it turns out, my fate has been much like that of the tragic figures of Lowell's own generation whom I have in the past spurned and abhorred. Perhaps all along I sensed that I was more like them than I could bear to acknowledge.

Lowell died in 1977, two years after I graduated from Harvard. He was returning from England, where his marriage to Caroline Blackwood had collapsed, to the safe harbor of Elizabeth Hardwick's apartment. He had with him a portrait of Blackwood, evidence that he could still be clueless and careless. He died of a massive coronary in a taxi cab. Like Odysseus, who is the subject in *Day by Day* of Lowell's last long poem, he spent most of his life between two worlds. Unlike Odysseus, he never quite reached home.

8.

I would like to leave the last word to Elizabeth Bishop, to whom I have been doing a strategic injustice in this essay, telling, as it were, only half of the story. Yet again it is time to correct an imbalance—this time one of my own deliberately perverse devising.

Bishop's last book, *Geography III*, is, even more than *Day by Day*, a quintessential example of the relatively rare, late-in-life flowering of a poet's imaginative powers. It also, no doubt, reflected Bishop's growth as a person, a growth perhaps facilitated by her last, most rewarding love affair, a seven-year relationship with Alice Methfessel, a bright, high-spirited, much younger woman. Bishop, as we now know, remained remarkably sexually active and vibrant virtually until her last day. The erotic remained as alive in her as it did in Lowell, though she continued to deem such matters too private to serve, except obliquely, as subjects of her poetry.

In the masterfully realized poems of Bishop's last volume, *Geography III*, human others appear with far greater frequency than in her previous volumes: in "The Moose," her fellow passengers, with whom she feels an evident solidarity; in "In The Waiting Room," her foolish aunt and her strange companions in what is a kind of holding pen; in "Crusoe in England," her vivid imagining of Crusoe himself as a real historical figure, beset by losses, missing his life stranded on another island, and particularly his more-than-mere companion, his beloved Friday, now deceased. In "One Art," Bishop at last comes to terms, if not quite triumphantly, with her tragic loss of Lota, a loss that can be partially mitigated by art when it is closely aligned with life and with the living of it. Finally, in the posthumously published "North Haven," she writes a loving remembrance of Lowell himself.

Again, as countless others have pointed out, a deep vein of feeling often lies behind or within Bishop's reticence and the hard-won elegance of her poems, which at their best approach a kind of perfection. Her perfection, however, is not cold; it intensifies rather than deflects our apprehension of feeling. Lowell's poems seldom reflect, are perhaps less interested in, this kind of impulse to achieve perfection. No matter. He mined, if imperfectly, other veins.

Bishop and Lowell, as suggested before, though linked as friends, were quite radically unlike each other as poets. They were, indeed, too unlike each other to be fruitfully compared. And yet each had a salubrious effect on the other. Bishop admired the "un-pulled punches," the frontal emotional attack of Lowell's poetry; Lowell admired the elegance, tact, and restraint of Bishop's poems, in which scarcely a word ever jars or is out of place. Bishop's influence served as a corrective to Lowell's occasional histrionics. In the last line of a late sonnet that is a kind of elegy before the fact for Bishop, Lowell writes of her "unerring muse that makes the casual perfect." In context, the term "muse" refers both to Bishop's own unerring muse and her service as a muse for Lowell. Lowell's work, in its turn, encouraged perhaps the increasingly frank pathos of Bishop's poetry, culminating in poems like the aforementioned "In the Waiting Room," "Cruise in England, and "One Art" in *Geography III*.

Ultimately, for all their differences, there was one crucial way in which they were similar. Bishop once wrote to Lowell that she was "the loneliest person who ever lived." When Lowell was asked what effect he wished his poems to have upon a reader, he replied quite simply that he wished to be "heartbreaking." I suspect that but for her reticence, Bishop would have given the same reply. Bishop would outlive Lowell by only two years. Always frail, she died suddenly of acute respiratory distress.

The structures of Bishop's poems, like the bay she describes in "North Haven," are reassuringly stable, but like the islands which the bay protectively encloses, and which she imagines as drifting, they do contain multiple slight shifts, "A little north, a little south, or sideways." The reference to *North and South*, the title of her first book, in the lines just cited is not accidental. The poem is not only a memorial to Lowell but a kind of *ars poetica* by a poet who was as self-consciously concerned with poetry as an art form as was Lowell.

"North Haven" enacts a kind of pilgrimage, a pilgrimage in the present that is also a pilgrimage to the past, to a seaside town in Maine in which Bishop had spent much time with Lowell. This return involves a kind of double consciousness like that Wordsworth in "Tintern Abbey." The poet returns in the present with a sense of loss but also a hope of possible compensation to a place that has meant much, and much that cannot now be recaptured, in the past. In Bishop's case, the compensation is nothing so abstract as Wordsworth's "philosophical mind," but takes the form of the renewal bestowed by spring, the season in which her pilgrimage takes place.

This renewal, ever new, ever the same, but never exactly the same, accommodating fine shades of difference like those so vitally apprehended by Bishop, can no longer be experienced by her sad friend, though spring reflects, and its song birds call to mind, the endless repetitions and revisions, rearrangements and sometimes derangements, of Lowell's work. But the songbirds, in fact, can only repeat, not revise, their five-note songs, just as Lowell's songs, having become immutable, can only be repeated, reread, recited, even learned by heart, but not without violence changed or revised.

And yet Lowell's poetry, though now unchanging, retains its pathos, fulfills its wish that it break our—its readers'—hearts. Bishop's reference to the sparrows' "pleading and pleading" that "brings tears to the eye" directly alludes to Whitman, to "Out of the Cradle Endlessly Rocking," likewise set by the sea, in which songbirds bring tears to the eyes of the child as incipient poet.

The poem, with its references to the renewal vitality of spring, to songbirds and flowers, conforms, though again casually, seemingly unselfconsciously, to the conventions of the genre of the pastoral elegy—while at the same time subverting them. In contrast to a natural world in which even islands are depicted as being in motion, and to the conventional elegy's promise of apotheosis, of a transformed life after death, Lowell has suffered a change that is perhaps the end of all change, a terminal stasis. And yet Lowell's poetry, unlike the poet, will have some kind of afterlife, will be received differently and afresh by its future readers.

Again, like many of Bishop's finest poems, "North Haven" begins with the apparently simple, with description and reminiscence, with the accurately noted and the vividly recalled, and then, lifting off, ends with revelation—even if, finally, all that can be definitively revealed in "North Haven" is the depth of Bishop's almost lifelong affection for Lowell, as well as the respect she felt for his art.

NORTH HAVEN

In Memoriam: Robert Lowell

I can make out the rigging of a schooner
a mile off; I can count
the new cones on the spruce. It is so still
the pale bay wears a milky skin; the sky
no clouds except for one long, carded horse's tail.

The islands haven't shifted since last summer,
even if I like to pretend they have—
drifting, in a dreamy sort of way,
a little north, a little south, or sidewise—
and that they're free within the blue frontiers of bay.

This month our favorite one is full of flowers:
buttercups, red clover, purple vetch,
hackweed still burning, daisies pied, eyebright,
the fragrant bedstraw's incandescent stars,
and more, returned, to paint the meadows with delight.

The goldfinches are back, or others like them,
and the white-throated sparrow's five-note song,
pleading and pleading, brings tears to the eyes.
Nature repeats herself, or almost does:
repeat, repeat, repeat; revise, revise, revise.

Years ago, you told me it was here
(in 1932?) you first "discovered girls"
and learned to sail, and learned to kiss.
You had "such fun," you said, that classic summer.
("Fun"—it always seemed to leave you at a loss. . .)

You left North Haven, anchored in its rock,
afloat in mystic blue. . . And now—you've left
for good. You can't derange, or rearrange,
your poems again. (But the sparrows can their song.)
The words won't change again. Sad friend, you cannot change.

A Note about the Author

George Franklin graduated from Harvard University, where he studied poetry with Elizabeth Bishop and Robert Fitzgerald, in 1975. He subsequently received an MFA in Creative Writing from Brown University and an MA in English Literature from Columbia. He lived for over ten years in the ashrams of his spiritual preceptor in India and in upstate New York. He has published two books of poetry, *The Fall of Miss Alaska,* Six Gallery Press, 2007, and the chapbook *Contour With Shadow*, Frolic Press, 2016, as well as a book of criticism, *Some Segments of a River*, published by Nicasio Press. His poems, including "Talking Head," a forty-page work in blank verse, have been published widely, most prominently in *Epiphany Magazine* and in *The Recorder, The Journal of the American Irish Historical Society*.

CPSIA information can be obtained
at www.ICGtesting.com
Printed in the USA
JSHW050804280722
28529JS00003B/100